Constituting Human Rights

What counts as ethical conduct in world affairs?

Global civil society and the society of democratic states are the two most inclusive and powerful global practices of our time. In this book Mervyn Frost claims that, without an understanding of the role that individual human rights play in these practices, no adequate understanding of any major feature of contemporary world politics from 'globalization' to 'new wars' is possible. *Constituting Human Rights* argues that a concern with human rights is therefore essential to the study of international relations.

Global civil society comprises those millions of people worldwide who claim first generation rights for themselves. By doing so they constitute one another as civilians. The language of rights used in this practice indicates that it is a practice that is open to all and without borders. Strikingly, the validity of claims made in it are not conceptually linked to any specific legal system or sovereign state. Within democratic states, however, the participants constitute one another as holders of citizenship rights, as people with a right to participate in self-government. Frost holds that the rights claims made in this practice are only real insofar as they build on the civilian rights of the earlier practice.

An understanding of the centrality of rights claims and the practices in which they are located provides a much needed guide to all of us concerned to understand contemporary international relations and concerned about ethical conduct in world affairs. This exercise in constitutive theory puts forward a powerful tool with which to tackle some of the pressing ethical issues of our time, such as those to do with refugees, asylum seekers, new wars, secessionist movements, international labour practices and many more.

Mervyn Frost is Professor of International Relations at the University of Kent at Canterbury. He was previously Professor of Politics at the University of Natal, South Africa and President of the South African Political Studies Association. His constitutive approach to international ethics was first published in *Towards a Normative Theory of International Relations* and reworked in *Ethics in International Relations*.

Routledge Advances in International Relations and Global Politics

Constituting Human Rights

Global civil society and the society
of democratic states

Mervyn Frost

London and New York

First published 2002 by Routledge
11 New Fetter Lane, London EC4P 4EE

Simultaneously published in the USA and Canada
by Routledge
29 West 35th Street, New York, NY 10001

Routledge is an imprint of the Taylor & Francis Group

© 2002 Mervyn Frost

Transferred to Digital Printing 2003

Typeset in Baskerville by Taylor & Francis Ltd
Printed and bound in Great Britain by Antony Rowe Ltd, Chippenham,
Wiltshire

British Library Cataloguing in Publication Data
A catalogue record for this book is available from the British Library

Library of Congress Cataloging in Publication Data
Frost, Mervyn.
Constituting human rights : global civil society and the society of
democratic states / Mervyn Frost.
Includes bibliographical references and index.
1. Human rights. 2. Civil society. 3. Democracy. 4. International relations.
I. Title.
JC571 .F6998 2002
323–dc21

2001058878

ISBN 0–415–27227–0

Contents

1   Introduction

In this brief monograph I argue that it is not possible to gain a proper under-standing of the international relations of our time without taking the notion of individual human rights seriously and that the acquisition of such an under-standing cannot be achieved through some simple process of observation, but requires of us that we engage in ethical argument about the proper place of human rights in our contemporary international practices. This involvement with ethical theory is not something we do *after* having come to grips in some direct 'empirical' and norm free way with the key features of how things stand in the practices of world politics, but is part of the very process required in order to understand our contemporary world. Insofar as effective participation in interna-tional relations depends on the participants having a proper understanding of the practices within which they are acting, an understanding of the place of human rights in these practices is a precondition for effective action in this domain. This kind of engagement with ethical questions concerning human rights is not something which may be confined to the specialists in the subfield of political ethics, but is something with which all participants in international rela-tions (academics and lay people alike) engage in some measure.

As will become apparent in the course of this monograph, determining the place of fundamental human rights in our contemporary global practice is not a simple task. There is no clear consensus on this matter amongst the participants in the practices. Indeed, in the discipline of International Relations (IR) the dominant view is that human rights are at best a marginal concern for those interested in understanding international affairs. A central aim in this work is to challenge this dominant position by showing the converse to be true, by showing, that is, that no proper understanding of our international practices is possible without at least some understanding of the central place which human rights play in them. But having said that, it remains to be shown what precise role concepts of basic human rights play in our contemporary global practice (or practices).

The object of my inquiry in this book is not some entity 'out there' that might be called the international system which I am intent on describing or explaining from, as it were, some external point of view. Instead, my point of departure (which I take to be relatively unproblematic) is that I, together with millions of other people worldwide, am a participant in certain practices which are global in their reach. The audience which I am addressing consists of my co-participants in these global practices. My goal in this work is to put before this audience a convincing understanding of these our common international practices that shows how human rights are intrinsic to them. In short, I write as a participant in these practices addressing my fellow participants.

I take my task here to be analogous to the following three scholarly endeavours. First, my task is similar to that faced by a theologian seeking to put forward his or her understanding of what is involved in being a participant in the practice of Islam, Judaism, Christianity, Hinduism, Buddhism (or some other religious practice) to fellow participants in the religious practice in question.[1] Second, it is similar to what a jurisprudent does when putting forward arguments about how best to understand a given system of positive law.[2] Third, my task is akin to that of a scholar putting forward his or her understanding of the practice of scholarship in general.[3] The features of these analogous cases which I wish to highlight here are: that the theologian, jurist and scholar involved in such debates all understand themselves to be addressing their interpretations of the practices in question to their fellow participants; that although there might be fierce arguments about rival understandings of the practices in question, throughout the process participants recognize one another as co-participants within a given social formation (the arguments are not addressed at outsiders with a view to convincing them of the desirability of joining some practice currently foreign to them); that clashes between insiders about the proper understanding of their common practice are likely to be extremely hard fought because what each is putting forward is a view which he or she hopes will become the dominant understanding within the practice and will become the guide to action for fellow participants.

Any attempt to offer a comprehensive understanding of a social practice must start with some assumptions about, references to, or outlines of, some set of ideas held in common by the participants in it. Indeed, it is not possible to understand the very notion of a practice without an appreciation that practices, by definition, consist of sets of people relating to one another in terms of commonly accepted ideas about what they are doing. This is a central insight of the *verstehen* approach to social scientific inquiry and has been discussed with great sophistication by, amongst others, W. Dilthey, Ludwig Wittgenstein in his later work, and Peter Winch.[4] It is also a central plank in what has come to be known in the discipline of International Relations (IR) as the constructivist literature, although many contributors to this literature still wish to maintain a mix of *verstehen*, empiricist and positivist approaches to IR.[5, 6]

It is a feature of interpretive analysis that all attempts to put together comprehensive accounts of a given practice always involve an element of circularity. This follows from the character of the activity. What we have in such analyses are participants putting to their fellow participants accounts of how the beliefs, ideas, constitutive rules, regulative rules, norms, maxims, and so on, of the practice under scrutiny fit together. In seeking to present a comprehensive understanding of a practice (be it a game, a church, a state or an international organization) an interpreter must necessarily refer to other features of the very practice under consideration.[7] Disputes about the proper understanding of a practice involve we who are participants in it referring one another to different features of our common practice – such disputes involve our putting forward rival accounts of how the components of the practice hang together or cohere. A typical claim in such an argument might be: 'No, that's not how I understand this feature of our practice; it clashes with the following commonly accepted aspects of our practice', and so on.

What I am setting out to do, then, is to put to you, the reader, whom I take to be my co-participant in important global practices, an understanding of these practices and the role which human rights considerations play in them. The test of the validity of that which I put forward here is valid or not will depend on whether you find that my account of the way in which the elements of our practice cohere fits with your best understanding of how they hang together.

Clearly key questions to ask here are: (1) are we indeed co-participants in global practices? and, if we are, (2) what are these global practices in which we are participating? These questions depend on having answers to two prior questions: (3) how does one identify the practices within which one is a participant? and (4) how does one distinguish between the discrete practices within which one participates? (How do I know where one stops and another starts?)

Here are two rough and ready answers to (3). First, one can identify the practices within which one is participant by noting the memberships one claims for oneself. Thus, for example, by claiming my membership of a family, a university, a church, a nation or state, I both presuppose and indicate to others the existence of the practices thus named. Second, one can identify practices within which one is a participant by noting what skills one claims to possess. Thus, for example, when I claim that I can speak English, play soccer, write and do arithmetic, each of these claims, if true, identifies me as a participant in a practice – those of speaking English, playing soccer, writing and doing arithmetic. At a very general level one may say that an examination of what I can do will indicate the practices within which I am a participant.[8]

The answer to question (4), about how to distinguish one practice from another, is that one does so either by noting the criteria insiders use to distinguish themselves from outsiders (for example, 'Our criteria for citizenship in this state are ...'), or by noting the full set of what is presupposed in claiming a skill at this or that. Thus for example, consider the previous list of skills which I claim for myself, that I can speak English, play soccer, write, and do arithmetic. In claiming that I speak English I am presupposing that there are others who can also do this, and I indicate that there is a range of things I am able to do within the language which are capable of being understood by other language speakers in this practice. These will include describing things, asking questions, giving commands, and so on. Entailed in this claim is the further claim that I have an adequate vocabulary, and so on. The limits of the practice of speaking English are indicated by what English speakers take as skills which are quite irrelevant to the claim that one can speak the language. Thus, it is typically held that being able to speak Zulu, being able to play soccer, being able to write and being able to do arithmetic are all skills which are not required in the practice of English speaking. A similar exercise can be gone through for each of the other skills which I claim to have. We identify the limits of the practices by noting what participants normally regard as skills that are irrelevant to one who claims participant status. In short, the borders of practices are defined by the participants.

Our global practices

It is clear that each one of us could draw up a long list of practices within which we participate. Typically each list would refer to participation in at least some of the following: families, schools, churches, social clubs, sports clubs, political parties or movements, commercial companies, trades unions, universities, men's clubs, women's clubs, and so on. Although the listed practices vary in size, it is clear that none of them is global such that it would be true to say that nearly all people everywhere are participants in it. So although it may be the case that most of us would consider ourselves a member of some or other family, we do not all belong to the same family (or school, church, social club, sports club, political party, commercial company, and so on). We who participate in these practices do not claim that all people (or even most people) are co-participants with us in these practices.

However, there are two practices within which I participate which are very nearly global in their scope. Both of these practices are such that I both know myself to be a participant in them, and, I know that most other people (if not all) are also participants in them. We can identify these practices by the claims that we make and the things that we do.

Let me start identifying these two practices by setting out of some of the claims which I make for myself. Readers may then decide whether they are also participants in these practices by simply determining whether they make the same kinds of claim for themselves. I identify these practices by determining who else agrees with me that they are participants in it. Those who agree are the audience to which this book is addressed.

Let me start with the straightforward assertion that I consider myself to have an equal set of fundamental human rights in common with other humans every-where.[9] I consider myself to have a right to free speech, to freedom of movement, assembly, contract, conscience, and the right to own property, and a right not to be killed and not to be assaulted.[10] Having these is basic to my conception of myself as an ethical being. Were they to be denied me I would consider myself the victim of a grave injustice. Furthermore, I believe that I may legitimately claim these rights wherever I find myself – as far as I am concerned they are valid in all places. These are rights I claim internationally. I do not confine my claims to some domestic arena within an established state. Thus, whether I am in Britain, Angola or on the high seas, I consider myself to have these rights. Of course, I know full well that not all people will respect the rights I claim for myself. There are many who might be tempted to abuse them for one reason or another.

Considering myself to be the holder of certain fundamental human rights is not something which I, at some point, chose to do and which I could stop doing at will. Understanding myself in this way is part of my self-conception – it is, if you like, a component of my identity.[11]

I must stress that my conception of myself as a rights holder is not tied to my being embedded in some or other legal system which is itself, in turn, embedded in a distinct territorial state. It may well be that the legal system, in the state within which I find myself, overtly protects the rights I consider myself to have. This is indeed the case in South Africa where I am at present. But were this legal system to collapse I would still consider myself to have these rights. My claim to the possession of these rights is not dependent on the existence, or not, of a legal system entrenching them and it is not dependent on my membership of some territorially defined state. As one eminent author puts it 'These rights are not derived from the citizenship of any country, or the membership of any nation, but are taken as the entitlements of every human being'.[12]

Beyond claiming these rights for myself, it is part of my conception of myself as an ethical being that I recognize all other sane adults as having the same set of basic human rights. As with my own rights, this recognition of the rights of others is not territorially confined. I recognize the basic rights claims of others wherever they happen to be. I respect them whether they find themselves in a state with a legal system geared to entrench and protect those rights, or whether they find themselves in a quasi state, a collapsed state, or in an area where there is no functioning state at all.[13]

I am not alone in claiming for myself a basic set of rights. Millions of people around the world make similar claims. They, like me, take themselves to have a set of basic rights which they may call upon wherever they are and whatever the condition of the political authority in their region. I am confident that the readers of this book, in like manner, are likely to consider themselves holders of fundamental rights. There are few people nowadays who do not claim for themselves at least some of the rights which I have listed. As evidence consider the following: every person who before 1990 understood him or herself to be part of one of the largest lobbies of all time, the anti-apartheid movement, had some conception of human rights and how these were being denied to the majority in South Africa. Every person who understands him or herself to be a citizen of a state which is a member of the United Nations organization probably has some conception of themselves supporting the human rights which are embedded in the UN Charter.[14] Every newspaper reader, TV viewer and radio listener who was outraged by the Tiananman Square massacre, the mass rapes in the Bosnian conflict, the genocide in Rwanda, the oppression of women in Afghanistan and the exploitation of child labour in Pakistan, is likely to have a sense of these being cases of human rights abuse. Indeed, most mass media report these events in the language of human rights.

Beyond the examples mentioned above which point to reactions that stem from a commitment to human rights, we can find similar behavioural evidence of a commitment to basic rights in many people's involvement in the global economy. Every person who buys or sells something, however small, in the global market place claims a property right for themselves in that which is being bought or sold and acknowledges the property rights of those with whom they are dealing. It would be very difficult for a person to act in a market without having a conception of being the bearer of some basic rights. Only people who consider one another to be rights holders can make contracts with one another.

It is important to note that people did not always consider themselves rights holders in the way that I have outlined. For long periods of history (indeed for most of recorded history) no market relations existed between property owners, on the one hand, and slaves, minors and women, on the other. Members of these latter categories of persons were not considered rights holders and could thus not be full participants in what markets existed in those times. There are still people who are not recognized as full participants in the global free market.

It is difficult for me to envisage a person who does not claim for him or herself at least some of the rights I have listed. Such a person would have to be one who said of what I am writing here, either, 'I don't know what is involved in claiming a right and thus I never do it because I do not know how', or 'Although I understand what claiming these rights for myself would involve, I nevertheless do not do so because I quite properly understand that I am without rights, I am a slave, a minion, a servant, a subject, a lackey of another who is my master, my lord, my owner.' As should be abundantly clear by now, to the extent that such people exist, this monograph is not directed at them. Instead, it is directed at the readers who claim fundamental rights for themselves and at that vast group of people worldwide who either explicitly believe they have a set of fundamental human rights or who act in ways congruent with such a belief.[15]

Of course, those many millions of us who see ourselves as the holders of fundamental human rights are not all agreed on what fundamental rights we have. There is often argument amongst us about whether the set of rights we take every person to have includes only the so-called negative liberties (such as the rights not to be killed, assaulted, tortured, the rights to freedom of speech, freedom of movement, freedom of conscience, to private property, and so on) or whether the list should be extended to include what have come to be known as 'second generation' rights, such as a right to health care, housing, education, an old age pension, an annual holiday, and so on. The picture is further complicated by those who claim that beyond these categories of fundamental rights we also have 'third generation' rights, such as the right to be a member of a self-determining nation or ethnic group encapsulated in a sovereign state. Not only are there arguments about different generations of rights, but there are arguments within each of these schools of thought about what rights should be included on the list for each generation. For my present purposes I shall not concern myself with the details of such disputes because I wish to address myself to the widest possible group of participants in the rights practice. This is that group made up of those who consider themselves to be holders of, at the very least, first generation rights. This is the largest group because it encompasses within it all those arguing for an extension to the basic list. Those who argue for positive rights (the welfare rights) do not, in general, argue that they have these instead of the negative liberties. Their case is that these are supplemental to the liberties (or are a necessary means for realizing first generation rights).[16]

The social whole within which I claim basic rights for myself and recognize them in others (independently of whether I or the others find ourselves in functioning states or not), I shall call *civil society*. This is a society without geographical borders – it is global in its reach. It comprises all those who claim basic rights for themselves and recognize them in others. Throughout this monograph then, when I refer to 'civil society' I am referring to the society of people who regard one another as holders of certain fundamental first generation human rights. That they do so is reflected in the way they speak to one another (and the way they speak about one another). Put another way, it is a community defined by the rhetoric it uses. We know the members of this community by the language they speak. Its members are those who use the language of basic human rights.[17] I shall elaborate on the major features of this society in Chapter 5.

It is important to stress at this point that amongst social scientists there is an ongoing and oftimes heated debate about the meaning of the label 'civil society'. For some theorists it points to that set of social entities which is neither a component of the state, nor a component of the global capitalist market, but may best be described as a set of autonomous social entities that forms a buffer between the power of states and the power of the market.[18] For others, civil society must be understood as a component of the capitalist market order.[19] My use of the term 'civil society' is not to be read as a contribution to this debate in political sociology.[20] Instead it is to be understood as the name which I use to label the society of people that make first generation rights claims for themselves. The parameters of this society are determined by the claims made by those of us who are members of it. This is a stipulative definition. The test to determine whether a person is a member of this society or not is found in his or her answer to the question: 'Do you consider yourself to have the following rights … (the list might include the right not to be killed, tortured, assaulted, the right to free movement, speech, contract, association, conscience, academic freedom and the right to own property)? This practice consists of all those who answer this question with 'I do'. This civil society consists of all of us who make these rights claims for ourselves.

In what I have said so far I must not be taken as claiming that the members of civil society, let us call them civilians, are all *ad idem* on what their membership of that society entails. We who claim to hold the rights of civilians in civil society argue with one another at length about what rights we take ourselves to have. Opinions on what to include on the list vary from minimalist to maximalist.

Beyond being a member of civil society, that global practice within which so many of us claim basic human rights for ourselves, I find that I and many millions of others worldwide make another set of rights claims for ourselves which demonstrates the existence of another global practice.

In order to identify this practice, let me, once again, start with a consideration of some claims which I make for myself. I claim citizenship rights for myself as a member of a sovereign state within the global practice of sovereign states. I notice that most other adult people in the world claim similar citizenship rights for themselves. Once again I am confident that the reader of this monograph is one of this group. By claiming these citizenship rights for ourselves we signify the existence of a global practice. As this practice is presently organized, we who are citizens of sovereign states, know that it is always appropriate to ask for the identity of the state within which a person claims citizenship rights for him or herself. It may sometimes happen that a person turns out to be a citizen in more than one state. But citizenship always implies membership of some or other state or states. In contemporary parlance the meaning of citizenship is logically tied to the notion of statehood.

My participation as a citizen within the practice of states is very important for me both from a practical and ethical point of view. Were I to be denied the status of citizen this would be a major ethical setback for me and, in all probability, it could be a major practical setback too. As a citizen I understand how denying this status to my fellow citizens would be a major ethical setback for them. I shall have more to say about the importance of the ethical status of citizenship in Chapter 6.

I am not merely a citizen within a system of sovereign states, but I am a citizen in a democratic state within a practice of democratic and democratizing states. This standing is very important to me from an ethical point of view and it is important to most others in the world who claim citizenship for themselves. Of course, not all states within which people claim citizenship rights for themselves are democracies, but it is important to note that the vast bulk of the existing states in the world today either are democracies or profess themselves to be on the road to a democratic form of government. In like manner, the vast bulk of people who understand themselves to be participants in states as citizens either do, in fact, enjoy democratic citizenship or they overtly aspire to do so.

Once again, I am not claiming here that all of us worldwide who claim citizenship rights for ourselves in the society of democratic and democratizing states are agreed on what citizenship rights are or should be. There are huge and ongoing disputes about what citizenship rights should be and about what would constitute a democratic state properly so-called. There are, for example, debates about the merits of unitary forms of state versus federal forms, about Westminster-style electoral systems versus systems of proportional representation, and representative democracies versus participatory democracy. But all these, I take to be, as it were, 'in-house' debates about what a well-organized society of democratic states should be like. These are debates between democrats within the broad practice of democratic and democratizing states.

My easy affirmation of my membership of what is for me an important global practice, the society of rights holders (civil society), becomes problematic when I attempt to reconcile it with my simultaneous membership of the other global practice I have identified – the society of democratic and democratizing states. The core problem is easily stated. The rights I enjoy in one seem to exist in tension with the rights I enjoy in the other. For the rights I enjoy as citizen require of me that I recognize that I have certain special obligations to my fellow citizens. Might not my allegiance to my fellow citizens lead me to privilege them at the expense of others, outside of this state, who are not my fellow citizens? Might it not, indeed, lead me to override, ignore or discount the civil society rights of those outside of the state in which my citizenship rights are located?

What makes the tension here particularly difficult to think about and solve is that rights are involved in both practices. Civil society I have defined as the society of first generation rights holders. But the democratic state (and the society of democratic and democratizing states) as I have described it, is also a realm of rights. The democratic state is a domain within which actors confer upon one another the standing of holders of certain fundamental democratic rights, the set of rights known as citizenship rights, which include, amongst others, the right to vote, the right to stand for governmental office, the right to form political associations (such as political parties), the right to subject the actions of governments to close scrutiny, and so on.[21] What we apparently have, then, is a major tension between these two global practices which comprehend just about everybody, everywhere. We need to confront the somewhat startling question: could it be that millions of us are participating in two global rights-based practices which are mutually contradictory?

In this book, then, I am addressing those men and women worldwide who, like me, claim first generation rights for themselves in global civil society and who claim citizenship rights for themselves in the society of democratic and democratizing states. In writing it, I have two specific goals. First, I wish to show that it would be very difficult, if not impossible, to understand any aspect of contemporary international relations without a full understanding of these rights-based practices in which so many of us are participants. Understanding individual human rights in their constitutive global practices is fundamental to any proper understanding of contemporary world politics. Second, I wish to consider in some detail the tensions which appear to exist between our commitment to the human rights of all in the context of global civil society, on the one hand, and our acknowledgement of the special claims of right made upon us by our fellow citizens in the context of our respective states, on the other. Put slightly differently, I am interested in determining whether one can coherently participate as a rights holder within both the global civil society of first generation rights holders, on the one hand, and in the society of democratic and democratizing states, on the other. This is an investigation into how, if at all, the fundamental ethical rights-based commitments we incur through our participation in these two practices cohere with one another (or fail to cohere).

The question about the coherence (or not) of these two practices is not merely of theoretical interest – not merely a question of interest to those of us with an interest in political philosophy. It is also of practical significance. The problem of coherence between the ethical commitments stemming from our simultaneous participation in these two practices becomes a practical problem when we find ourselves having to consider what to do about a whole range of burning issues in the world today. Such dilemmas confront us whether we are policy makers in positions of high office or whether we are merely ordinary men and women going about our everyday lives. Let me simply list for my co-participants in these global practices several issues which press in on me in this way. In doing so I am confident that these (or very similar ones) are felt as urgent by many of my fellows who claim these rights for themselves – who claim, that is, both first generation rights and the rights of citizens.

The dilemmas of civilians and citizens

I am not a major actor in international relations, but like most people I regularly find myself having to decide what to do about a number of difficult ethical matters with an international dimension.[22] My decision more often than not is to opt for inaction, but this, too, is a decision and as an ethical being I am responsible for it. Often in the process of deciding what to do (or what not to do), the basic tension mentioned above comes to the fore, although it takes on different forms. The basic tension in each of the following examples appears to be that between privileging my rights as citizen at the expense of my commitment to fundamental first generation rights for all, or, what amounts to the same thing, privileging the requirements of the society of democratic and democratizing states over those of global civil society. Below are examples of different manifestations of this tension as I experience them.

I am a South African citizen and I value my citizenship rights. I enjoy the benefits which citizenship brings me. But I am not cocooned in my state. Beyond the ethical problems which arise in South Africa, problems concerning reconciliation, restitution, redistribution, liberty, equality and human rights, to mention but a few, I regularly recognize a range of ethical problems which arise beyond the borders of South Africa. Here I have in mind problems such as those posed by:

- poverty in neighbouring areas (Should not I as an individual, or my church or my state, do something about redistributing resources to the needy elsewhere in Africa?)
- economic refugees from poor states bordering South Africa who are seeking entry into South Africa – the situation in the states of origin often appears hopeless (Should we citizens of South Africa not allow some migrants in to seek work in our comparatively vibrant economy?)
- simmering civil wars in some states in the region, Angola, Democratic Republic of Congo, Rwanda and Burundi (Should I support intervention by the South African military forces or even intervention by private armies based in South Africa?)
- the absence of democracy in many Southern African states and the general abuse of human rights taking place throughout the continent (Should I, or

my state, or an international organization, intervene, by force of arms if necessary, in order to remedy these ills?)

Although I am not, as an ordinary citizen, in a position of great power to do much about these matters, nevertheless, I am not powerless. Various courses of action are open to me. For example, as an academic I could use my position to advocate certain courses of conduct to those with social and political power; I could write advocacy articles in scholarly journals and the popular press; I could join international agencies directed towards alleviating some of the more pressing problems (agencies such as Amnesty International and Human Rights Watch); I could set up (or take part in) fund raising activities, the product of which could be used to make a contribution to solving the problems in hand. If many other people joined me in concerted action we could, together, bring considerable pressure to bear on key actors across a range of issues. We could lobby our governments and political parties to implement specific policies; we could seek to bypass the state and take action via NGOs which might be locally based or international; we could act by seeking to influence public opinion locally and abroad; we could lobby churches with global reach, and so on.[23]

Before doing any of the above, I and others who claim rights for themselves have to decide what to do. We have to answer the question: What ought to be done? It is in seeking an answer to this question that I encounter the persistent ethical problem to which I alluded above and which may be restated as follows: As one with the rights of a citizen in a democracy I believe that both I and my government are ethically entitled to devote our resources and energies to securing the best interests of South Africa and its citizens. Yet, at the same time, believing as I do, that all people have a fundamental set of equal human rights within the practice of global civil society, it is plain to me that paying attention to the human rights of those beyond South Africa's borders will require of me (and my fellow citizens) that we devote rather less attention to our own self-interest and more attention to the interests of those beyond our borders whose rights are being abused. There seems to be a major tension between what I am entitled to do as a holder of citizenship rights in the practice of democratic and democratizing states, on the one hand, and what is required of me as a member of the wider community of rights holders in global civil society, on the other. How should I think about this matter? Am I entitled, in terms of my citizen's rights, to demand that the government of my state pursue the interests of this state, even when this will be at the cost of civilian rights beyond the borders of my state? Or should I, as one who respects people's civilian rights (both within the borders of my own specific state and beyond its borders), uphold these even in those cases where doing this would be at some cost to my own state? The default option, the one which comes about when I choose to do nothing about migrants, about huge refugee problems in central Africa, about civil wars nearby, about starvation not far from South Africa, and about genocidal campaigns in neighbouring states, and so on, has the effect of favouring the 'my state is primary' position at the cost of the 'protect the fundamental basic human rights of all' option. Although I usually choose the default position, I am left with a nagging feeling that there may not be good reason for this choice, that I (and many other South Africans, probably a majority) are guilty of ethical turpitude in acting this way. In this book I attempt to think through this problem.

I have sketched the ethical tension which I feel between the rights which I have as a South African citizen and those which I have in the wider community which stretches beyond South Africa's borders. There is little doubt that the same kinds of ethical problems confront citizens in other democracies. That citizens of other democracies express sharp concern at news reports of genocide, mass rape and torture in the areas beyond the borders of their own states, indicates their application of ethical judgement to the events taking place there. This has happened with regard to events in Somalia, the former Yugoslavia, Palestine, East Timor, Rwanda, Burundi, Democratic Republic of Congo, and others. But, here again, the tension alluded to reappears for those advocating action to prevent these things. Here, too, as citizens, they often come to face an uncertainty about the ethicality of incurring expenses abroad for large-scale military, humanitarian and/or reconstructive intervention in foreign places, while the ethical claims of fellow citizens are still unsatisfied. This reluctance is not merely based on the naked self-interest of the citizens in their own state, but on an ethical judgement that intervention would be wrong; the judgement that, in the first place, our ethical concern ought to be focused on the well-being of our own state (and its citizens). Others ought to be left alone to be self-determining in their respective states.

The present work, then, is at one and the same time an analysis of the ethical features of two major global practices within which nearly all people participate in one way or another, and it is a work in applied ethics focusing on a particular set of ethical problem cases which many of us have encountered in international affairs. In particular, it explores the ethical relationships which hold between two major practices of our contemporary world order: global civil society, on the one hand, and the society of democratic and democratizing states, on the other.[24] More specifically, it examines the role which ideas about human rights play in both of them.

This work is an elaboration of a theory on which I have been working for some time. In an earlier work I outlined an ethical theory which I called the constitutive theory of individuality. I now wish to make use of constitutive theory to analyse the two practices mentioned.[25] A central thread in all that follows is that much current thinking about the place of human rights in world politics is based on a series of misunderstandings about the architecture of these two practices, their relationship to each other and the place of rights in the structure of each.

Defining ethics

In writing this monograph I have, as an explicit goal, to establish the centrality of ethics for the study of international relations in general. Before closing this chapter let me briefly outline in an introductory way what I understand by ethics. I shall do so by contrasting ethical problems with technical ones.[26]

In the normal course of our activities in the international domain (and in the other domains of our lives) we regularly confront two very different kinds of problem. Many of the decisions which we have to make in the international realm (and the acts which follow from these) are *instrumental*. They call upon us to decide on the best *means* for realizing the goals which we happen to have. How might Turkey best protect its national security? How might we South Africans maximize our international trade? How might Real Madrid set about winning the European Cup? What equipment should a particular multinational corporation buy to achieve its goals? In seeking to solve the problems of nuclear fusion what experiments should international scientists set up? Given my tastes where should I take my holiday, should it be Greece or Turkey? How should the UN be reorganized in order to make it more effective? All of these are examples of instrumental questions.

In seeking answers to instrumental questions we turn to modes of inductive reasoning in an effort to find out what policies have worked in similar cases in the past. Extensive data banks on comparable cases would be essential to this type of inquiry. We often set up experiments to determine what works best given the circumstances.

Over and above these, there is another class of problem which we regularly confront in the international sphere. These are what I call *ethical* problems. Here are but a few examples of the kind of problems I have in mind (note that all these problems may be seen as problems for individuals or as problems for political leaders):

- A British citizen who is a member of the Palestinian diaspora living in London has to decide whether to volunteer his or her services to a militant nationalist movement fighting for a free Palestine.
- A South African (or British, or French, or ...) citizen who has to decide whether to vote for a party whose policy is to be tough on immigration.
- A runner who has to decide whether to buy running shoes from a company that makes use of child labour at the point of manufacture.
- A holidaymaker who has to decide whether to take her holiday in a state which abuses human rights (such as Turkey)?
- A person who has to decide whether to support movements in support of global free markets or not. (A recent form of this question is posed to those wondering whether to support policies aimed at structural adjustment in Third World states.)
- A person in a developed state confronting the decision whether to speak, write, vote or campaign for active intervention in collapsed or collapsing states (in places such as the former Zaire, Angola, Somalia and Mozambique)?
- People in traditional tribal practices confronting the decision whether to support the policies of their governments which threaten the survival of such practices.

- A person considering whether actively to seek to bring an end to certain cultural practices in societies other than their own – such as, for example, the practice of female genital mutilation.
- People called upon to respond to the genocides they have become aware of (such as those which took place in Rwanda, Burundi, or Zaire, as it was then called) or to the ethnic cleansing which took place in the new states which emerged from the former Yugoslavia.
- Those considering what to do about famine in distant places.

In all these cases the people confronting such problems (be they doing so as individual men and women, or as political leaders) may well decide to do nothing, but even doing nothing will still have been an ethical choice and their inaction will have been a deed in world affairs.

What is the distinguishing mark of the question: 'What is it *ethical* to do under these circumstances?' *In this book I take ethical decisions and the actions which flow from them to be decisions and actions which are judged by the extent to which they meet the constitutive norms within a given practice.* Ethical problems, then, are those which arise with regard to the interpretation and application of such constitutive norms. Some of the most pressing and intractable ethical questions arise when the constitutive norms of one practice come into conflict with those of another. All of the examples which I have chosen in the list presented above are of this kind. What then are constitutive norms?

Constitutive norms are the norms within a practice, adherence to which is required of anyone wishing to be considered an actor in good standing within that practice. This somewhat turgid statement is easily illustrated. A constitutive norm of the Christian practice is that one should love one's neighbour, of a nationalist practice that one should love one's nation above other social formations, of academic life that one should pursue truth and not propagate falsehood, of most games that one should not cheat, and of the interstate practice that states should not commit acts of aggression against other states.[27] These norms are constitutive in that failure to abide by them is taken as an indication that the actor in question is no longer to be considered a participant in good standing within the practice in question. Thus, for example, Christians who fail to love their neighbours, nationalists who betray their nation, academics who propagate falsehoods, sportsmen and women who cheat, states which seek to undermine the system of states (and so on), are all guilty of flouting constitutive rules within these practices and are thus guilty of ethical failures. They have transgressed rules which are so fundamental to the practice in question that adherence to them is considered a *sine qua non* for anyone seeking to be a participant in good standing within that practice. A failure to abide by the constitutive standards of a practice raises the question whether the actor in question really is entitled to recognition within the practice as a Christian, a nationalist, an academic, a sportsman or woman, a sovereign state, and so on. It is clear that this kind of failure stands in sharp contrast to failures which are merely of a technical means/ends nature.[28] Thus, a Christian who fails to realize his short-term strategy of making money for the church, a nationalist who fails to organize a successful rally, a sports person whose strategy fails to win the game and an academic who fails to solve a problem in his word-processing software, none of these impinges on the actor's standing within the practice in question. These are merely failures to use the appropriate means to bring about a desired goals. They are merely instrumental failures.

It follows from this account that ethical criticism cuts deeper than instrumental criticism. Within those practices which I have been using as illustrations, it is, for most participants, of fundamental importance that they not lose their standing as members – it is important to them not to be expelled from such practices for being un-Christian, a traitor to the nation, a cheat in sport, a fraud in academic life, and so on. At the limit, falling foul of the constitutive standards in these core practices – which, by definition, leaves us open to ethical criticism – exposes us to possible 'excommunication' from the practices in question. To be criticized as having failed in some matter of instrumental reason is one thing, but to be subject to ethical criticism for contravening the constitutive rules of a practice or practices which is/are important to us is an altogether more serious matter.

For the most part, in our daily routines within practices, both local and international, (whether they be families, corporations, states or international organizations), staying within the bounds of the constitutive rules and by so doing behaving ethically, poses no particular problems for us. In the vast majority of cases, whoever we are and wherever we find ourselves, we know how to behave in accordance with the constitutive rules of the practices within which we participate and by so doing avoid ethical criticism. Of course, that we know what the constitutive rules require of us, does not signify that we shall indeed do what they dictate.[29] All of us are often guilty of backsliding, which exposes us to ethical criticism. In general, though, we know what is required of us by the constitutive norms of the practices within which we participate. We thus know how to avoid ethical criticism. No agonizing takes place, none is called for, and no expert ethicist is needed to guide us on such matters.

We all participate in many different practices which have an international dimension to their activities. Our everyday conduct within these is normally straightforward. We know what the constitutive rules require of us, we act on this knowledge and we avoid opening ourselves to ethical criticism. Thus, to mention a few examples, when we maintain a friendship with others in different parts of the world (France, Argentina, Japan, Nigeria, etc.) we experience no particular problems with regard to the proper standards of conduct required within the practice of friendship (we know what is required of us to maintain our standing as friends with such foreigners). When we participate in sport with others from elsewhere in the world we know how to act to avoid ethical criticism (we understand what would count as cheating and what would count as disgraceful conduct). In our international meetings of Christians (Muslims, Jews, Hindus, and so on) we know what counts as behaviour appropriate to our being a Christian (Muslim, Jew, or Hindu). In like manner, the states to which we belong, for the most part, know what counts as appropriate conduct for an actor constituted as a state in the system of states – they are clear about what would count as wrongdoing by one state against another. Whether the state be Saudi Arabia or Belgium, those who govern it know, for the most part, how to avoid the charge of wrongdoing in international affairs. They keep their treaty commitments, avoid armed aggression against other sovereign states, respect the rights of foreign diplomats, co-operate with international organizations attempting to alleviate suffering caused by international disasters in far off places, and so on. To repeat the central point: in our daily routines within those many practices which have an international dimension, we generally know what is to count as conduct in accordance with the constitutive rules of the practices in question and thus as conduct which will not be subject to ethical criticism.

Hard cases

For the most part then we follow the constitutive rules of all these international practices as a matter of course. We do it without giving any overt thought to ethical matters. But this is not always the case. I wish to highlight two circumstances in which ethical problems surface. The first happens when, within a given practice, it is not clear what conduct the constitutive rules prescribe. This happens when new circumstances present themselves to the participants. The invention of the atom bomb presents a pertinent example here. Other examples might be the invention of birth control pills, which presented a set of overtly ethical problems to most established global religions, and current developments in genetic engineering, which pose interesting ethical problems for all those involved in the use and distribution of seed and livestock worldwide.

A second kind of hard case for ethics emerges when what is prescribed by the constitutive rules of one practice within which we participate appears to clash with the constitutive rules of another practice within which we are active. All the examples which I listed above fit into this category of hard case. In this book I shall focus on what I take to be the major contemporary example of this kind of hard case for ethics – the apparent tension between civil society, the practice within which we constitute one another as holders of first generation rights, on the one hand, and the society of democratic and democratizing states, the practices within which we constitute one another as the holders of citizenship rights within democratic states, on the other.

In summary then this book is addressed to those many people worldwide who, with me, consider themselves to be civilians in global civil society and as such the bearers of first generation individual human rights, and who, at the same time, consider themselves to have (or at least aspire to have) citizenship rights in a democratic state in the practice of democratic states. It is addressed to the many who, like me, find themselves confronted by a somewhat excruciating ethical puzzle which is that the constitutive rules of global civil society seem to be pulling us in a strikingly different direction to the constitutive rules of the society of democratic and democratizing states.

2 Individual rights in world politics

Central not marginal

In the opening chapter I argued that when faced with the imperative of action in international affairs we, who consider ourselves rights holders, often find ourselves confronting difficult ethical choices. Many of these, I pointed out, seem to arise from an apparent incompatibility between what is required of us in the practice of rights holders (civil society) and what is required of us as members of the system of democratic and democratizing states.

A typical set of such ethical problems which we encounter might include the following:

- Refugees: Like all people, refugees and migrants have a set of fundamental basic rights which includes the right to freedom of movement. Yet we seem to act contrary to this right when we acknowledge that sovereign democratic states may legitimately close their borders to refugees and migrants.
- Nationalism: Ought we to support nationalist movements (individuals freely associating around cultural icons) in their quest for self-determination (the people of East Timor, for example) if the majority in such movements are engaged in curtailing the liberties of other people (the so-called 'minorities') in their areas?
- Secession: What is the ethical way to think about the problem of secession (a problem made urgent with the break-up of the Soviet Union)? On the one hand, we acknowledge that states have a right to maintain order and to protect their own citizens within their sovereign territories (by force if necessary), while, on the other, we acknowledge that individuals may use their right to freedom of association to form national groups which may wish to secede from the state within which they presently find themselves.
- Global distributions (maldistributions) of resources, technology, education, wealth, etc.: With regard to these we recognize that individuals may use their rights to live their lives as best they can, yet their ability to do this appears to be infringed by sovereign states which often block their access to resources, job opportunities, and so on. States do this by erecting border controls. Yet we acknowledge that the first duty of states is to look after the interests of their own citizens. This often seems to require that outsiders be denied access to certain key resources.[1]

- The environment: Are we (whoever, and, wherever we may be) entitled to impose environmentally sound policies on people beyond the borders of our states even where these infringe their individual freedoms (such as their freedom to use their property as they deem fit and their freedom to be self-determining within their own states)?[2]
- Genocide: In the face of a genocide may the international community impose policies on a majority group within a given territory or would this be infringing the pooled individual rights of the majority in that area to be self-determining?
- Famine: If it can be shown that the policies of sovereign democratic states have the effect of bringing famine to people in far off places, does this not infringe at least some of the rights of the famine-stricken individuals? It may be said to deny those individuals the very preconditions necessary for their enjoying even their basic negative liberties.
- Civil war: When a civil war rages within states it is likely that individual human rights will be abused by both sides. Does the international community of rights-respecting people have a duty to intervene to protect human rights or should it respect the right of the states in question to non-interference in their domestic affairs?
- Abuse of power: When the government of a sovereign state abuses the rights of its own citizens, do outsiders (individuals or states or other forms of organization) have a right to intervene to protect those individual rights?

Many people feel, as I do, a degree of ethical puzzlement about some of these issues (and no doubt about many others issues which I have not mentioned). That we feel a sense of ethical bewilderment in each of these cases indicates both that we take individual human rights seriously, and that we take the rights of states seriously (the latter being the expression of our citizenship rights). It is because we are in earnest about individual rights that we are horrified by ethnic cleansing in Bosnia, by genocide in Cambodia and central Africa, by brutal treatment of political prisoners in Turkey, by torture wherever it occurs, by the denial of rights to women in many places, by sex tourism from Western Europe to (amongst other places) Thailand, and by the exploitation of child labour in Pakistan. Similarly, it is a consequence of our taking the rights of democratic and democratizing states seriously that many in the international community objected so strongly to the denial of citizenship rights to South African blacks during the period of apartheid, that some of us are shocked by the denial by Israel of democratic statehood to the Palestinians, by the invasion of the sovereign state of Kuwait by Iraq, that we feel equivocal about the interference by one state in the domestic affairs of others, and so on.

If I am right that many of the issues (disputes, conflicts, problems) in world affairs must be understood (wholly or in part) as arising from a concern about human rights in civil society and citizenship rights within democracies, then it is quite remarkable to find when we turn to the discipline of International Relations (IR) that human rights are treated as being of only marginal significance. They are seen as being peripheral to the explanation of the main systems, processes and projects within the sphere of international affairs. Why? In this chapter I seek to do two things. First, I seek to explain why IR as a discipline has not placed human rights as a central focus of its endeavours. Second, I argue that those in the mainstream of the tradition who are guilty of this failure have misunderstood the role of human rights in the practices of world politics today. Far from it being the case that understanding the place of human rights in contemporary global practices is marginal to the central concerns of IR, I argue that *no satisfactory understanding of the two major practices of contemporary world politics is possible without a proper understanding of the place of individual human rights within them.*

Rights at the margins of the discipline

In the teaching of International Relations and in the scholarly writing within the discipline, the discussion of human rights is generally introduced at the end of the courses taught and in the closing chapters of the books written for those courses. Often the topic is not introduced at all. Whether the teacher is a realist, pluralist, structuralist, critical theorist or post-modern theorist (or one of the majority, who teaches a little of each, without endorsing any), it is always thus. Evidence for this is to be found in almost all introductory textbooks. Here are three selected from my shelf at random: in Richard Mansbach's *Issues and Actors in World Politics* he discusses 'The state versus the individual: Human rights in the global arena' in the penultimate chapter.[3] Richard Little and Michael Smith in their *Perspectives on World Politics* include, after thirty-three chapters, two chapters dealing with normative issues, neither of which is explicitly about rights.[4] In Paul Viotti and Mark Kauppi's *International Relations Theory: Realism, Pluralism and Globalism*, the last two chapters deal with normative issues, but here again there is no section on human rights.[5] The curricula of universities offering courses in IR also support the point I am making. Courses on human rights are increasingly being offered to students, but always as 'add on' modules after the core courses have been taught. Such optional modules are often classed together with other supposedly peripheral (not central) topics such as feminist approaches to IR, normative theory, and theories on international relations and the environment.

At first glance it may seem as if there are good reasons for relegating rights to the bottom of the academic agenda, the end of core texts, and the margins of taught courses in mainstream IR. It may seem as if those who busy themselves with the study of human rights in world politics are active on the 'soft' margins of a discipline which has a clear 'hard' core. In a world still struggling with the problem of war, both within states and between states, in a world where terrorism is used by many movements in pursuit of their goal of national liberation, in a world in which advanced industrialization seems to be threatening the prospect of future life on the planet and where an AIDS epidemic threatens the whole continent of Africa, it may well seem as if a concern with individual human rights is somewhat frivolous. Such an interest might seem akin to a scholar in strategic studies developing a research interest in military etiquette. Although etiquette may be a worthwhile area of study, it is clearly subordinate to the study of how wars – classical, civil or guerrilla – are fought, won or lost. Of course, in its own right studying military etiquette may be interesting. But it is clearly subordinate to the primary purposes of armies. For patently the consequences of winning or losing wars are great for all concerned and research projects which do not focus on explaining war itself do, indeed, seem rather trivial.

That the study of rights is marginal to the main concerns of IR seems to follow from the fact that states and their governments are the key actors in world politics. This is a view which is held not only by members of the different realist schools of thought in IR, but applies also to the 'English School' and to liberal approaches to the discipline. The differences between these schools turn on rival accounts of the role of states in world affairs. They all accept that it is possible to understand and explain the major role of states in the international system without particular reference to individual human rights. Such theories take it as obvious that states are in the first place preoccupied with the maintenance of their territorial sovereignty and with the maintenance of order between sovereign powers.[6] On this view, the maintenance of human rights is at best of secondary concern.[7] In spite of a growing interest in ethics in international relations, this is still the picture accepted by the majority of scholars in IR.[8] There is, one might say, a realist norm underlying the whole discipline.[9]

It may not be surprising to find that realists in IR take this position with regard to the place of human rights in understanding global politics. It is surprising, though, to find that this view is also accepted by those few scholars in IR who are, indeed, interested in human rights. They, too, see states as central to world politics as it is currently practised. Rights, in their view, are neglected in the practice of world politics and reforms are necessary to accord them their proper place. Their theoretical work is aimed at contributing to this reform process. We may say that their concern with human rights is, in a sense, heroic. They wish to bolster the case for human rights in a world of states which they understand to be largely hostile to the idea.[10] Such human rights theorists find themselves in the same boat as animal rights activists (and the so-called 'Greens') who bravely put their case against the majority view. One might say, metaphorically speaking, that scholars from these schools preach righteousness in a world of sinners. The literature produced by these rights 'missionaries' refers to the great documents which have been adopted by states, to the mechanisms which have been put in place to get the ideals of the declarations made real in practice, it recounts the successes and failures of these efforts and, finally, the literature makes suggestions about how human rights in the future may be defended more effectively in this hostile environment.

In the conventional view which underpins the writing of even those who are sympathetic to human rights, the background is widely understood as follows: states may pursue human rights goals, but when these conflict with their vital interests then these interests will be accorded priority and will override the human rights concerns. A rights focus is seen as somewhat idealistic and not in accordance with a 'real' understanding of what the primary goals, motives and imperatives of states are.

What are we to make of this view of the place of rights in world politics? In a world of states, are individual human rights luxuries ('nice if you can get them'), which are secondary to the primary functions, interests and imperatives of states in their relations with one another?

In what follows, I develop in greater detail an argument sketched in the first chapter. *I make the case that a focus on human rights is not a secondary activity for scholars interested in world politics, but that, on the contrary, in the contemporary world, it is difficult to make any sense of international relations without giving proper attention to human rights.* My aim is not an attempt to foster a human rights culture in a world of states which is hostile to them; my aim is to make clear that human rights are already central to the practice of world politics as we know it. They (rights) are embedded in the practices of world politics in a way that cannot be ignored or marginalized by scholars in IR (or anyone else) insofar as they seek a proper understanding of what is happening in this domain. There is no defensible 'mainstream' way of tackling the subject of international relations which can succeed without giving prominence to human rights. Any explanatory model of international relations, which does not take the role of human rights in world affairs seriously is a flawed model and cannot explain how the international system works.

These are seemingly extravagant claims for which I shall provide backing in due course. Before doing this though, I wish to explain briefly why the 'rights-at-the-margins' view of human rights in IR is dominant in the discipline today. In order to do this I must start with a rough-and-ready indication of what I mean when I refer to individual human rights. [11]

In common parlance, several distinctive kinds of claim are referred to by the term 'right'. The similarities, differences and relationships between them have been neatly laid out by Hohfeld.[12] Whenever a claim of right is made it is a claim made within a normative practice. In the paradigm case, to claim a right is to claim a domain within which one is free to act, and with regard to which others have a duty not to infringe the area of freedom in question. A rights claim is a property claim in the sense that only the owner of the right may waive it.[13] Thus, for example, where I have a right to freedom of speech, it is my decision alone whether to use it or not under a given set of circumstances. Crucially, rights do not feature prominently in all social practices. In slave-owning societies slaves have no rights; in some societies women are considered to be without rights, and in many societies children have only limited rights.[14]

To claim a right (to freedom of speech, for example) is to give a reason to others not to interfere with one's speaking. The 'I have a right' type of reason for action is considered to have overriding weight. This reason for action may not be overridden by other reasons people may put forward for denying you this realm of freedom. In the example which I have given, having a right to freedom of speech amounts to presenting others with a weighty reason for letting you have your say. This reason outweighs other reasons which they may offer denying you this. For example, some may put forward as a reason for preventing you articulating your right-wing views that granting you this would contravene the will of the majority. In a rights practice a valid claim of a fundamental right to freedom of speech trumps this argument, even if it is the case that the majority of people would, indeed, think it good that you be silenced. It is often said that possessing a right is like holding trumps in a game of cards.[15] Thus even though the majority might want you silenced, you trump their majoritarian argument with one referring to your right to free speech.[16] Rights claims are, metaphorically speaking, often put forward by a David against a Goliath. Where rights are claimed, individuals are, more often than not, confronting giants of one sort or another. These might be those more senior than the claimant, those more powerful, those more numerous, or those more articulate or more vociferous. Rights claims are claims which the weak may use against the strong. Thus, in a rights practice a single dissident may assert his or her rights against a national or international majority. Illustrative of this was the civil rights movement in the USA where individuals from a minority group claimed their rights against the more numerous, more powerful, and institutionally better placed majority in the USA. In the light of this characterization of what is involved in having a right, it is now clear why struggles to actualize human rights claims are often presented as being heroic struggles.

Reasons for the marginality of rights in the discipline of IR

There is a whole set of reasons why individual human rights, at first glance, might seem to be marginal to the mainstream concerns of IR. These reasons do not all fit into a coherent package. Taken together, though, the arguments all push in the same direction.[17]

The dominance of the realist paradigm in IR

First, the dominant paradigm in IR is the realist one.[18] The premises, maxims, methods, values and traditions of this approach all militate against understanding the place of human rights in world politics in anything but a secondary position. The key tenets of realism are well known. The realm to be studied is made up of a world of sovereign states each of which must be understood as being preoccupied with its own security. These states are not subject to any comprehensive higher form of government, but relate to one another in terms of their perceived self-interest. The relationships between these states is determined by the power which each state possesses and the key to the power calculus which each makes is the military power it has at its disposal. In seeking their security, states, if they find themselves lacking in power, will resort to the making of alliances with other states and out of this process there will emerge balances of power. When these break down wars may occur.

According to this model, the empirical objects of study are the relations which states have with other states. What is of particular importance are the power relations which hold between them. According to this model, it may well be the case that individual states from time to time show some interest in human rights, but this should not lead us to shift our focus from the primary determinants of what happens in the world. These all have to do with states and power.[19]

Built into realist theories are certain 'value slopes'. Although such theories might profess not to be overtly concerned with normative issues, there is nevertheless a normative component within them.[20] With regard to normative issues, state-centric theorists are primarily concerned with the value of *order* and the preservation of the system of states. The preservation of these is understood to be a precondition for all the other values which people might hold dear.[21]

The realist paradigm with its focus on sovereign states relating to one another in terms of military power clearly does not build in a concern with individual human rights at a primary theoretical level. This is not to say that realists might not be interested in human rights as a secondary interest. Once order has been established in international relations, then the way is open for a concern with human rights. Once the order precondition has been met, then, on the realist view, we might turn our attention to investigating how human rights might be protected in a system of sovereign states. We might find that, on occasion, states collectively spend time and effort setting up co-operative endeavours – such as the United Nations, for example, which has as one of its specific goals the protection of human rights. But, at base, such activity is conditional upon the primary task which states have which is to maintain order. Many people (whether they be scholars or not) understand the place of human rights in world politics in this way.

Dominant understandings of political power in relation to human rights

The realist understanding of what power is and how power relates to individual human rights militates against taking rights as central to the study of global politics.

Implicit in several versions of realism is the idea that one only really has a right insofar as one has the power to enforce that right. Within fully formed states there is a concentration of power at the disposal of the government of the day and it can use this power to enforce the rights which individuals may be thought to have.[22] On this view it follows that, whereas, within states the study of human rights would be a sensible activity, in international relations, since there is no centralized rights enforcing power, human rights are unlikely to be realized in practice. Therefore one ought not to waste time studying rights in this realm.

There is a further point to be made here. In IR, theorists have often concentrated on the most dramatic of all threats, viz the use of military force. Clearly power understood as the ability to threaten a military sanction is something which can be used for good or evil. Here, once again, power, understood in this way, is ethically neutral. It is something which may be studied prior to and independently of human rights. On this view, a primary task for IR theorists must be to study power itself – how to get it, who has it, how to resist it. Only after completing this phase of analysis need one turn one's mind to questions about how those who have power ought to use it. But, as we have seen, even when realist theorists turn their attention to the uses to which power may be put, their concern is likely to focus on the value of order rather than on the values associated with human rights.

There is a second influential understanding of power in IR which we need to consider. This is what Steven Lukes has famously called the three-dimensional view of power, or structural power.[23] On this view, power is not akin to a weapon at someone's disposal. Rather it is something which exists, as it were, 'in the system'. Structures of power within a given social system constrain behaviour in certain ways. Two well-known examples of such structural theories are Kenneth Waltz's neo-realist theory of international politics and theories of imperialism such as Lenin's.[24] Consider the latter. Lenin argues that where people are engaged in a capitalist economy certain things will come about without their necessarily willing those outcomes. For example, monopolies will emerge (that is, capital will concentrate in fewer and fewer hands). Markets will shrink. The monopolies will seek new sources of raw materials and new markets in which to sell their products. The states which are home to such monopolies and which depend on them will come into competition with one another. This will result in the outbreak of wars. War can thus be explained, not in terms of what some one person willed, but in terms of the outcome of the operation of the system taken as a dynamic whole.

Waltz in like manner explains outcomes in international relations in terms of the unwilled result of a series of actions within a system. He describes the core components of the system as sovereign states seeking to maintain their sovereignty in an anarchic order. The power structure of the anarchic system constrains what the component states can do.

Scholars working with structural theories which explain large events in terms of the power which the structures impose on the actors, and where the actors in question are large collectivities such as capitalist monopolies and/or states, will regard any interest in individual human rights as secondary to their primary concern – the study of the structure of the international system. On this view the effects of the grand structure on micro units (individuals) within the system may be an important thing to study, but the study of these depends on the prior study of 'the laws of motion' of the grand structures themselves. What happens on the human rights front will be subordinate to the great movements of the forces of history.

The dominance of legal positivism

A further reason which leads IR theorists to view human rights as somewhat marginal is the dominance within the discipline of a particular understanding of law in general and international law in particular.[25] This view of what law is is known in jurisprudence as *legal positivism*.[26, 27] According to this view, a law is a command backed by a sanction. Law-abiding behaviour is what people do when they obey generalized commands because they fear the sanctions which will follow if they fail to obey the articulated rules. Let us examine the central tenets of legal positivism more closely as they apply to the laws *within* a given state.

The central idea is clear: the defining feature of legal rules (laws), as opposed to other kinds of rules, is that laws must be understood as the commands of a sovereign legislature and these commands are backed by the strong arm of the state's enforcement agencies. Thus the law obligating me to pay my taxes is a law because it is in the form of a generalized command from the sovereign law-making body. If I disobey its command I shall be brought to book by the police and judicial system. Applying this understanding of law to the international sphere immediately presents us with a problem since, of course, there is no sovereign legislator with power to back its commands.

It is easy to see how this understanding of law might influence thinking about rights in both the national and international sphere. First, within the domestic sphere any talk of individual human rights must be understood as merely the expression of ideals until such time as these are transformed into legal rules by a sovereign power with the might to enforce its will. Second, within the international sphere, since there is clearly no sovereign with the might to enforce his or her will on all people everywhere, all talk of there being individual human rights which are applicable globally must once again be understood as the expression of the ideals, hopes or wishes of the speaker in question rather than as a reference to something real in the world.[28]

There is a further implication of legal positivism which we need to consider. For positivists law is a command backed by a sanction, but it is more than this. Not any command backed by sanction will produce a law. Only those which are issued by a sovereign (or which can be ultimately traced to a sovereign) have this effect. The sovereign is an ultimate command-giver at the peak of a pyramid of command-givers. Thus the bye-laws of a town council are valid because they are authorized by the county council. In turn the authorizations of the county are authorized by higher bodies up a pyramid of authority which ends with the national legislature. This is the sovereign in that there is no higher law-giver than this. This is the body which controls the greatest sanctioning power in a state. On this view, my right to free passage through the streets of a town derive ultimately from the sovereign legislature. If some claim of right cannot be supported by an organogram which shows the hierarchy all the way up to a sovereign then, on this view, I do not have a legal right and I do not therefore have a real right. If I claim such a right then I am merely expressing an ideal or a wish. Once again we see here the close link which is taken to exist between having rights and having power. Transposing this way of thinking about rights onto the realm of world affairs it becomes plain that the absence of a sovereign global power indicates an absence of any real human rights in the global context. Talk of human rights must be understood as indicating a set of ideals, aspirations and hopes. Investigating these is a fit subject for visionaries and dreamers, not for realists whose focus is on the world as it is.

Rights and civility: the Hobbesian view

There is a widely held view about the links which hold between rights and civility which seems to undermine our taking rights in IR seriously. According to this view, it does not make sense for us to suppose that we have rights unless we live in some kind of society. In the absence of society, we would simply be confronting one another as naked power holders. Under such circumstances, commonly referred to as the 'state of nature', talk of rights would make no sense for, by definition, we would be under no system of common rule. Disputes would be settled by resort to the instruments of force such as clubs, swords, guns, bombs, and so on. From this view, talk of rights would only make sense were we all to become participants in some sort of civil society. Hobbes, the most important proponent of this point of view, thought that there were only two possibilities with regard to this matter. We either live in a state of nature, which is an uncivilized condition in which life is likely to be 'nasty, brutish and short', or we live in a social order that has been civilized by *law* understood in the positivist sense. Such a civil society can only come about through the creation of a sovereign who must have sufficient power to enforce its commands. The kind of power which is relevant here is the power of the sword. In Hobbes' view, if there is no sovereign, then we are still immersed in a state of nature within which there can be no security. In particular, there cannot be that kind of security which we have when we have rights under law – that is, rights backed by the command of a sovereign with military might at his shoulder.[29] Here again we see the link between rights and law which we discussed in the previous section. There can be no meaningful talk of the protection of rights unless there is law. And there can be no real law in the absence of a sovereign power.

When we apply this view of civil society to world politics it is, once again, quite clear that, since there is no sovereign power, therefore, by definition, there is no civil society. It therefore follows, once again, that talk of human rights is somewhat premature until such time as an international sovereign is established.[30]

Relativism

The factors undermining a serious concern with human rights in international relations discussed above are further complicated by certain philosophical positions which are currently in vogue.

It is widely recognized that there are a whole range of different moralities existent in the world. Often these are linked to established religions. Thus, there are Christians, Jews, Muslims, Hindus, and the moral codes associated with these. Furthermore there exist many secular moral belief systems, be they socialist, communist, or anarchist. Beyond these there are also any number of esoteric cults. When it comes to comparing these religious, secular- and cult-based codes with a view to establishing which value system is 'true', there is now considerable support for the view that there is no rational way of deciding which of these is in some ultimate sense 'true'. There is no single universally accepted set of criteria in terms of which we could make convincing judgements between these. This has lead to a widespread acceptance of *moral relativism*, which I here simply define as the belief that although we might argue the merits of particular points *within* a moral practice (Christians may argue whether birth control is in accordance with the scriptures or not; Muslims may argue about what the Koran prescribes with regard to the treatment of women, and so on), there is no way of arguing the merits of whole practices vis-à-vis one another. There is an absence of a universally accepted foundational framework from within which such an argument could be launched.

These insights have been greatly reinforced by the development of post-modern philosophical theories about the structure of knowledge. A defining feature of these is their commitment to anti-foundationalism. We are not in a position, say the post-modern theorists, to evaluate different discourses (including moral ones) in terms of some final grounded discourse because none such exists.[31, 32]

What precisely is the implication of relativism with regard to our discussion of human rights in international relations? What it implies is that what rights you think you have will depend on what morality you subscribe to. Any arguments we may have about rights must, on the relativist view, be arguments within an agreed-upon moral framework. Thus, if one is a liberal one may argue from within one's liberal moral framework about what rights prisoners-of-war have. Whereas, if one were a Muslim one would have to debate this issue from within an Islamic framework. But what is not possible is to make judgements about the relative merits of each of these frameworks taken as a whole. This is not possible because there is no overarching common framework from within which this could be done.

A further implication of this line of reasoning is that when it comes to choosing between practices it simply does not make sense to say that the choice is rational – it must be based on something else, such as, for example, personal taste. On this view we simply *choose* our moral practices. All of this suggests that in a world of many ethical systems a concern with universal human rights seems somewhat far-fetched.

The implications of relativism: imperialism or tolerance

It is worth mentioning at this point that the relativist insight discussed above may lead theorists (like you and me) in two diametrically opposed directions, both of which have implications for how we think of human rights in world politics.

First, we may reach a realist conclusion such that, since there is no way of rationally judging between any two moral frameworks (such as rights-based ones and their rivals), the only way of settling a dispute between them is through a power struggle. Such a struggle may lead to victory, defeat, or a midway position which is a balance of power. The opponent, on this view, is not judged according to some standard of moral worth (by definition the relativist cannot make such a judgement), but is judged as being simply 'other' and, as such, a possible threat to one's own values. Here we are back, face to face, with a realism which has no fundamental place for a theory of human rights. If a liberal state which believes in rights sets out to impose its version of human rights on other peoples, nations and states, then we must say (according to this view) that this is straightforward cultural imperialism. It is a case of the powerful imposing their ideas about human rights on the weak.

Second, the relativist insight might suggest to us that the appropriate response for relativists would be to adopt an attitude of tolerance towards those moralities which are at odds with ours. This is the typical liberal reaction – based on the principle that if we have no set criterion by which to judge the 'other' and his or her beliefs about rights, then we should at least give the 'other' the benefit of the doubt and leave him or her well alone. It is easy to move from this insight to one which stresses that the system of states, as we currently know it, is a system in which an array of different kinds of societies are contained within an ordered structure. Thus, we should respect this order and not meddle in the internal affairs of other states because doing so would be intolerant of the ways in which others differ from us. Ironically, this liberal response feeds back into the realist paradigm in that it suggests the desirability of a world of sovereign states in which the non-interference rule ought to be well observed. A world of sovereign independent states can be seen as a world in which diversity is respected. But even on this liberal account, there is but a limited role for human rights in world politics. Human rights may well be articulated, nurtured and protected within a given society or state, but, because of the relativist premise which underlies this particular liberal response, the argument cannot be made that human rights ought to be made applicable to all people. Once again the problem is the absence of the overarching framework.

Rights and special obligations

Finally there is a well-known problem in moral theory the nub of which concerns the suggestion that in our moral concern for others we ought to give special concern to those nearest and dearest to us, to those, that is, in our immediate communities. Many (if not most) people believe that the moral bonds which obtain between me and my family, or me and my nation, or me and my fellow citizens are more important than those between me and those more distant from me. Thus, if I have a choice between doing my duty with regard to my family and doing it with regard to a stranger in a foreign land, I ought to choose the former. These obligations are known as special obligations.[33] This line of thinking clearly has pertinence to the problem of human rights in international relations. For, if we accept a theory of special obligations, then we have a duty to protect the rights of those closest to us in our families, nations or states.

We should give preference to these over duties to protect the rights of those more distant from us. The prevalence of this way of thinking about the scope of our moral concern provides yet another explanation for the marginalization of human rights concerns within the discipline of IR.

Rights as central to understanding of contemporary international relations

I have made the claim that within the discipline of IR those concerned with individual human rights are considered to be working in an outlying field of the discipline and I have offered what I believe to be a set of plausible explanations for this state of affairs. Yet in spite of its apparent plausibility I believe this position to be based on a profound misunderstanding of the place of rights in world politics. Let me now present and defend a quite different view of the place of individual rights in the theory and practice of world politics.

In what follows I shall defend the strong claim that *no proper understanding of international relations is possible without knowing something of the place of individual human rights in the two key practices of world politics which I have identified.* These are global civil society, on the one hand, and the system of democratic and democratizing states, on the other.

In world politics today the notion of individual human rights is internally related to the other elements of the practices in which they feature. In order to make clear what is meant by 'internally related' an analogy is useful here. Rights are internally related to the other key elements of the two key practices in world politics we shall be looking at, in much the same way as 'making a run' is related to the other major elements of the game of cricket such as 'bowling a ball', 'taking a catch' and 'getting a batsman out'. Another set of internal relationships holds between the concept of 'scoring a goal' in the game of soccer and the other central elements of that game such as 'committing a foul' or 'being offside'.[34] It is not possible to understand the game of cricket unless one understands what is involved in 'making a run'. Once one understands what the relationship is between 'making a run' and the other elements of cricket, one can then go on to seek explanations for particular outcomes. It is important to notice that it follows from this that it is only possible to understand the practice of cricket in a *holist* way. It is not possible to understand one aspect of the game without linking it to the other core rules of the game. In order to understand what is involved in 'making a run', one needs to know what a batsman does, and what a bowler does and what a fielder does. One also needs to know what 'being in' is and how one ceases 'being in' and is got 'out.' To repeat, these concepts hang together as a whole which needs to be understood *in toto* before one can be said to understand the game. In like vein, I shall be arguing that an understanding of the practices of contemporary world politics requires some knowledge of the idea of human rights and how this relates to other central ideas of the two central practices we shall be examining in the rest of this book.

In what follows I am presuming that understanding must precede explanation.[35] What I mean by this is as follows. Once the rules of a practice as a whole are understood, we are in a position to identify particular events within that practice as being of this kind rather than that. Having done this we might move on to the subsequent task of explaining an event or set of events within the practice in question. For example, once we have understood that a given meeting is a summit meeting between heads of states (rather than a cabinet meeting, a round of wage negotiations, a caucus meeting of a political party, or a strategy meeting between allied military leaders), we might set out to explain why the meeting is taking place now instead of at some other time, why the agenda is what it is, rather than some other agenda, and so on. But it is always the case that before we can explain why an act is taking place (or has taken place) we need to identify the act as one which fits some description within the context of the practice within which it is being conducted. This requires an understanding of the practice as a whole.

I shall now defend the claim that understanding international relations as it is currently practised requires of us that we understand the place of human rights in the two practices which I have identified. Such understandings must be had prior to any attempt to explain particular events, such as the outbreak of this or that war, the occurrence of an armed intervention, the emergence of an arms race, the persistence of a long period of peace, and so on, through the long litany of topics which are customarily of interest to IR specialists.

Rights as internal to international political practices

What I now have to show is that the notion of human rights in these two global practices is linked to the other core notions of these practices in a set of internal relationships, such that if someone did not have an idea of what rights are and how they work in relation to the other elements of the practices in question, that person would be unable to comprehend these practices at all.

Let me put this to the test by listing a typical set of such subjects which IR theorists might consider worthy of explanation.[36] I shall first consider some actions which have to be understood within the system of democratic and democratizing states. Typical of what IR theorists might seek to explain in this domain are:

- the outbreak, conduct and conclusion of the Gulf War against Iraq
- the international dimensions of the internal wars in the states which comprise what was Yugoslavia
- the relations between the great concentrations of economic and political power in the states of North America, the European Union and those on the Pacific Rim. (And, of course, the relations which hold between all of these and that emerging economic and political giant, China)
- the international ramifications of the internal political and economic turbulence within Russia.

I could continue this list indefinitely, but I take it that these are examples of what would normally be considered important issues in the domain of contemporary world affairs.

My claim then is that none of the above can be understood (let alone explained) without the inquirer having some understanding of the rights of the citizen and how these relate to the other elements in the practice of democratic and democratizing states.

Consider the events in Kuwait in 1990. All the accounts of what happened in the desert identified what happened there as an instance of war. We were not simply told blandly that there was 'some violence' (some shooting, some bombing) taking place in a given geographic area. From the outset what the participants were doing was much more clearly identified as a specific action taking place within a well-understood practice. All the participants in this practice of states understood what was going on. They understood that here was an instance in which one particular actor, the state of Iraq, stood accused of wrongfully invading the territory of a neighbouring state, Kuwait. Furthermore, they understood that the United Nations (itself a collective actor comprised of states) and a majority of states from the community of states had condemned this invasion as in breach of international law. This majority understood from the outset that it was attempting to expel the wrongdoer by means of force. This right of Kuwait not to be aggressed against (which is embodied in international law) itself is understood, in the modern world, to derive from the rights of the individuals in a particular area, in this case Kuwait, to be self-determining. This right of individuals to be self-determining is expressed/embodied in the citizenship rights of individuals within sovereign states.[37] To repeat myself, in the face of this aggression against a sovereign state (which right is derived from the citizenship rights of individual men and women within its territory), the international community of states thought itself justified in attempting to expel the invader by means of force.[38] Saddam Hussein, the President of Iraq, understood what I have put forward here, although he disputed the charge, claiming that the war was an instance of US imperialism.[39] Of anyone who did not understand what I have set out here (and there may be such people), we would say that they had failed to understand the events in question.

In the world today the rights of states to be self-determining (to be sovereign, if you like) are understood to derive from the rights of the people within the given area to democratic government.[40] Even where democracy is not yet established, or where it is not yet to be found in its mature form, we understand that states are granted autonomy in order that a democracy might be established there in due course. Thus new states seeking admission to the UN system have to demonstrate their democratic credentials. No political entity with a basic constitution which established a racially determined minority rule (such as pertained in South Africa under apartheid) would be recognized as legitimate in the contemporary practice of states.

The international system was not always like this. For long periods of history, states (and the people in them) were understood to be the property of the monarchs who ruled them.[41] Without a grasp of the notions of 'monarch', 'realm' and 'subject' it would not be possible for us now (or for the participants then) to understand the international practice of absolutism. That was the way things were then. They are different now. Nowadays we cannot understand the international practice of sovereign states without understanding that the right of states to non-interference in their domestic affairs stems from the right to self-rule which individuals in those areas are taken to have. The right to self-rule is to be exercised by the state through the mechanisms of democratic government.

Knowledge of rights is not only needed to understand what the war against Iraq was about, it is also needed it to understand the conduct of the war itself. During the course of the war there was much discussion about the rights of non-combatants. For example, there was considerable media and political attention focused on a bomb which destroyed a shelter protecting women and children. Similar media and political attention was paid to atrocities which were allegedly carried out by Iraqi troops against Kuwaiti civilians. The only way in which anyone can/could make sense of these allegations (and the controversies and resultant policy decisions which followed them) is for them to have a detailed conception of what rights non-combatant citizens are deemed to hold in times of war. The history of the conduct of the Gulf War cannot be written without knowledge of these rights claims.[42, 43]

Finally, with regard to the ending of the war, it is not possible to understand what factors influenced the decision to end it without having a concept of the rights which the soldiers of the defeated Iraqi army were deemed to have. Many argued that the slaughter of fleeing soldiers on the so-called 'highway of death' was unjustified in that it infringed the rights of soldiers in a defeated army – it was contrary to the international law governing the conduct of war. Public pressure in this direction, it would seem, influenced the US government in its decision to end the war when it did. However, not everyone agreed that the high-tech slaughter of the fleeing soldiers was a policy which should have been halted when it was. Some thought that the long-term citizenship rights of the Iraqis would best be protected by persevering with the war until the whole army had been effectively destroyed. This, they argued, would free the Iraqi people from the tyranny of Saddam Hussein. It opened up the possibility of them enjoying citizenship in a functioning democracy. I do not wish to take sides in this dispute. What I want to stress here, though, is that both interpretations of this event (the killing of those who were fleeing along the 'Highway of Death') presuppose that the interpreters had knowledge of the rights claims of individuals which are relevant here.

It is important to stress once again that I am not suggesting that all observers agree with the rights-based interpretations of the events which I have put forward here. Some would, no doubt, claim that what transpired was an instance of US-led imperialism. They might claim that all talk of acting in the name of democracy and human rights in such cases is mere rationalization. These kinds of claims though are usually offered as counter-claims to the interpretations which I have put forward. Such counter-claims presuppose an initial under-standing of the rights-based account of the practice in question.[44]

Once the events mentioned above have been described, they clearly still need to be explained. What led Saddam Hussein to attack when he did? What factors produced the military strategy pursued by the allies? What different groups within the top US decision-making mechanisms brought about the decision to end the war? The production of explanations for these events and the writing of the full history of the war all presuppose an initial understanding that the state of Iraq had aggressed against the state of Kuwait which had a right not to be aggressed. This right itself is understood to be derivable in the final instance from the individual rights of Kuwaiti people to govern themselves. Furthermore, the events in the war (and what people said about them) could only be understood by those who know that even in war non-combatant women and children have rights which may not be infringed. Similarly comprehending the end of the war involved knowledge of the rights of defeated soldiers.

We turn now to the events in what was Yugoslavia – events which have resulted in so much misery over the last five years. Here, too, it is the case that before any explanation can be provided of what happened in that region, some initial identification must be made of that which needs to be explained. Doing this requires an understanding of the practices in which the actions were located. Just about anyone who reads a newspaper regularly (or who watches TV or listens to the radio) would be able to provide this. He or she would tell us (in more or less detail) about the wars which have been waged by the armies of different ethnic groups each claiming its right to be self-determining within a specific region. The wars were being fought over disputes about who was entitled to live where and under what government. He or she would inform us that the key antagonists have been the Serbs, Croatians, Bosnians and Kosovan Albanians. There are further sub-formations such as Serbian Bosnians, Croatian Bosnians, Serbian Kosovans, and so on. Individuals in each group have been claiming a right to be self-determining together with the other individuals in their ethnic group.[45]

In the battles between the 'nations' of the region, major disputes have arisen between the members of the groups in question and between them and the United Nations about the treatment of individuals. In particular, there have been a series of controversies and interventions around the issue of human rights abuses, such as those which occur in ethnic cleansing operations, mass rapes, mass killings, the systematic use of torture and other such atrocities.[46] Each of these abuses involves the idea that those being mistreated have a right not to be abused. Here again I am not claiming that all people agree on what rights individuals have, or that they agree on whose rights were in fact being abused in specific cases. There are clearly ongoing disputes about these matters. What I am claiming, though, is that without *some* understanding of practices within which individuals claim rights, what they are and how they fit into a wider practice or practices, it is not possible to identify the events which are to be explained by those who are expert in the politics of the region.

As I have indicated, in seeking to understand these events it is not merely the notion of rights which must be understood, for, as is always the case in social practices, a core element has to be understood in relation to all the other core components of the practice in question. Thus, in this case ideas about rights are bundled together with several other notions to form the wider practices of international relations. In order to understand the practice as a whole we need to understand all of these and the interrelationships which hold between them. Consider the Yugoslavian case; besides needing to understand the concepts of individual human rights, we need to have some understanding of the notions of state, government, nation, self-determination, democracy, sovereignty, and of the non-intervention rule, to mention but a few of the other core elements in this practice. It is only after we have understood these and after we have some rough idea of how these correlate with one another that we shall then be in a position to identify a series of events as that set of actions which comprised 'the wars in erstwhile Yugoslavia'.

Subsequent to having identified these actions, we might then go on to look for explanations for specific items amongst them, such as: 'Why did nationalism come to the fore only now and not earlier?' 'What factors brought about the break-up of multi-ethnic communities which had been living together in comparative harmony for decades?' 'Why have armies in this region of the world committed so many atrocities such as rape, the massacre of civilians, torture, and so on, rather than make use of other methods of combat?' 'Why did the Dayton Peace Accord succeed where earlier attempts at securing peace had failed?'

Having shown how some knowledge of individual rights is required for an understanding of events within the practice of states, let me now turn to a typical list of some events in contemporary global civil society which we might wish to explain. Here, once again, I shall seek to show that these cannot be understood, let alone explained, without us having some notion about individual human rights and the practices within which they are located. Consider the questions:

- What is globalization?
- What impact will the spread of the market to China have on the form of government in that country?
- Will the spread of the market economy in Africa increase or decrease the possibility of viable democracies there?
- What will the political consequences be of the rise and expansion of new social movements?
- What impact will economic refugees have on the current practice of inter-state politics?
- What will the political consequences be of the rise of global pressure groups such as Greenpeace, Amnesty International, Human Rights Watch, etc.

Here, once again, in order to comprehend any of these events we need to have some notion of human rights. Consider the first item on the list: 'What is globalization?' No sense can be made of this assertion unless one has some idea about what the market is. In order to do this one has to have some notions about individual rights in relation to certain other key concepts. In particular, one needs to know something about individual rights to private property, the right to form associations (companies, multinationals, and so on) and the right to make contracts. In order to understand what a market is we need to know at least that it is an arrangement within which people, who understand themselves to have the right to own commodities, buy and sell these to one another.

As I mentioned earlier, the operation of the market involves more than property rights. It requires a far more comprehensive set of rights. A player in the market needs to be able to gain access to information about what is happening in the marketplace; thus he or she needs a right to freedom of speech and freedom of information for himself – or herself – and for other players in the marketplace. Beyond this he or she needs to be able to associate with other property owners to form companies of one kind or another. This requires that the players have a right to free association. In order to be efficient companies in the marketplace the players need to have a right to freedom of movement and freedom of association, and so on. They need this in order to get their products to those who would buy them. A market without such freedoms would not work. I repeat my central contention which is that an understanding of the market presupposes that one understands what individual rights are and that one knows something about how the different rights relate to one another to constitute this social practice as a whole.

Turning now to the penultimate item on the list which concerns the phenomenon of economic refugees. Before we can offer any explanation of this phenomenon we need to have a concept of individual human rights and the practices within which they are located. In order to make my point, consider the following deliberately far-fetched examples of what would clearly be misunderstandings about refugees. The Mozambican migrant problem in down-town Johannesburg, South Africa, is not properly understood, if such people are comprehended as creatures who have burst through the perimeter fences of South Africa and who now need to be eradicated. The problem is also not properly understood as a case arising from the arrival of an excess number of tourists from Mozambique for whom suitable accommodation needs to be provided. Both of these 'understandings' simply miss the central point. In order to comprehend the problem as one concerning illegal economic migrants, we need to have a notion of a sovereign state with the right to police its borders, but we also need to know that trespassers (such as the migrants whom we are considering) have certain rights simply because they are human. In terms of these rights we know that it would be inappropriate to cull them, exterminate them, enslave them, or imprison them. In short, then, to understand the problem of economic migrants requires of us that we understand both that sovereign states have a right to determine what is to count as an illegal border crossing, and that we understand that those who cross borders maintain certain basic human rights irrespective of whether they have arrived legally or not. It is because of the tension between these two sets of rights that migrants pose such a difficult ethical problem for us. If migrants were considered to be rightsless people, the kind of problem they pose for states would be completely different. For then it would be appropriate to treat them as vermin. States would merely be confronted with the technical problem of finding the best way to eradicate them.

Once we have *understood* economic migrants in the way outlined above we may then proceed to seek *explanations* for sudden increases in the flow of such migrants, for the success of certain anti-migrant policies (as opposed to others), and so on. Here, once again, the central point is clear. Having a conception of the illegal migrant problem rests on our having an understanding of social practices within which the participants are understood to be the bearers of fundamental human rights.

Concluding remarks

In this chapter I have outlined the ethical tension between individual rights in civil society and citizenship rights in sovereign states which I believe is encountered by many people in present day international affairs. Since this tension seems to underlie many pressing international problems of our time, I turned to a brief consideration of the discipline which might be thought best placed to offer guidance about how to understand and react to this set of tensions – I turned to the discipline of IR. What emerged is that although there is nowadays a sub industry within IR which focuses on human rights in the international domain, the interest in human rights is still understood to be marginal to the discipline's main concerns. I then described the ways in which the currently dominant approaches to IR marginalize a concern for human rights and I outlined the reasons which account for these dominant views.

In the concluding section I made the case that most of the actions we seek to explain in world politics can only be understood within social practices which have as a central component a concern with individual human rights. Thus anyone who wishes to understand our contemporary world has to have some in-depth knowledge of how ideas about individual human rights fit into the two major practices of our time.

In the following chapters I shall examine in some detail these two global practices and the relationships which hold between them. But before doing this I offer an addendum to this chapter which outlines the ways in which my inquiry about human rights differs from several traditional approaches to the topic. This section is a diversion from the central argument and may be skipped by those who wish to stay on the highway of my argument.

A short addendum

Constitutive theory and human rights: bypassing induction and metaphysics

Part of my project in this book is to bypass a number of intractable problems which preoccupy scholars examining human rights in international relations and to suggest an alternative way of examining the place of rights in our current practices of world politics. The intractable problems arise at the end of the following line of argument:[47]

The language of human rights suggests that each one of us is born with a specific bundle of rights. We have these rights simply by virtue of our being human. They are natural rights. The rights we are born with give us a standard by which we can determine whether specific acts, policies, pieces of legislation, institutions and constitutions are justified or not. If any of these overrides our individual rights as humans, then they are unjust and we have good ethical reason to oppose them. These natural rights are to be distinguished from legal rights which we have within legal systems of positive law. It is important to distinguish between these categories of rights (natural and positive) because, according to the theory of human rights, the rights we have by virtue of our humanity, our natural rights, are standards we may use to criticize positive law.[48] They are prior to positive law.

It is at this point in the story that the intractable problems emerge. It is obviously important to ask here: 'How do we know that all people have these rights?' and 'What rights do people naturally have?' These questions are asked because people often engage in disputes about precisely what natural rights people have. The well-known debates about first, second and third generation rights are examples of this.[49] These questions are difficult to answer because what rights people 'naturally' have cannot be determined through any process of simple observation (their rights are not attached to them like limbs – open for all to see), and because, as I have already mentioned, we cannot definitively determine what rights people have by referring to legal textbooks for we often wish to use natural rights as a set of standards by which to judge whether laws within a legal system are just, or even whether a whole legal system is just or not.

How then might we determine what natural rights people have? One approach might be to examine empirically all known societies with a view to determining whether there might be in each one certain common features – certain common principles of morality from which we could then derive a rights-based theory.[50] We might find that all societies place some restrictions on the taking of life, on sexual conduct, and on the control of property. Although it is the case that most societies do, indeed, have constraints in place on these three activities, this does not take us very far for the content of the restrictions varies greatly from society to society. Consider the diverse range of responses to polygamy, abortion, infanticide, suicide and war found in present-day societies. Furthermore, any commonalities that are found are likely to be too general and too bland to provide the kind of 'critical edge' we expect from rights-based theories. The first intractable problem then is this: to even the most casual observer of history and of the world we live in today, it is clear that not all societies have as a component of their cultures the same ethical system of rights. There are starkly divergent views on ethics in different societies. This suggests that all talk of basic or natural rights must be culturally specific. No process of induction across diverse cultures will show that all people have the same natural rights.

An alternative approach to these difficult questions has been to claim that human rights may be revealed to us by reason. Grotius spoke of natural law (from which theories of natural rights have been derived) as the dictate of right reason. This is a defining feature of the approach used by natural lawyers. A long tradition of such reasoning is to be found within Roman Catholicism. An influential present-day contributor to this tradition is John Finnis.[51] In IR theory Michael Donelan has been a staunch supporter of natural law as applied to international politics.[52] The difficulty with such an approach is immediately apparent. What if my 'right reason' delivers a different answer to the question 'What rights do people have?' to your 'right reason'? What if my view of what accords with reason differs from what others believe? Those who hold that they know what reason dictates must *a fortiori* claim that those who see things differently are backward, uneducated or blinkered by some ideology. Their reason must be flawed. Those who are labelled in this way (as having flawed reason) will, of course, view those labelling them thus as arrogant and high-handed.[53]

It is easy to see how scholars in dispute with one another about the nature of 'reason' will soon find themselves dealing with the most fundamental issues of philosophy – issues that deal with the foundations of knowledge itself. Rights theorists pursuing this track soon find themselves asking whether there is a universal reason which will reveal what rights all people have, or whether 'reason' itself is culturally determined and varies across societies and historical periods.[54] Immanuel Kant sought to find the transcendental categories of thought itself, to find out what was presupposed in all thought. Post-Kantians, taking their lead from the later Wittgenstein, have argued that reason and thought must always be understood as being relative to specific cultures. If one follows this tack, it negates the guiding idea that all people are born with the same reason which will reveal to them that they have the same set of natural rights. What are taken to be one's natural rights will be determined by the culture of the society within which one lives.[55] The second intractable problem, then, may be stated thus: the search for the foundation of rights in 'right reason' quickly leads theorists to the domain of 'high philosophy' (a domain once known as 'metaphysics') in which what has to be confronted are questions about rationality, epistemology and ontology. The debates in this sphere have been conducted for at least two thousand years and there is little reason to believe that they are about to be definitively settled. The debates in metaphysics take place between well-entrenched philosophical schools of thought, which include empiricism, rationalism, idealism, transcendental philosophy and philosophical realism.

In this book, I aim to bypass both of these recurrent problems. I aim to avoid both the hitherto fruitless search for what is common to the practices of Christians, Muslims, Jews, Atheists, Hindus, New Age believers, nationalists, Buddhists, animists (and so on through the hundreds of different social practices both past and present), on the one hand, and the endless debates in the upper reaches of abstract philosophy in which idealists do battle with realists, Aristotelians confront Platonists, the rationalists confront ordinary language theorists (and so on through the long list of philosophical schools of thought), on the other.

In the previous chapters I have set out the beginnings of an argument about the place of human rights in world politics which does not depend on unearthing some hitherto elusive commonalities across different societies and does not depend on bringing the debate about the great issues in philosophy to a successful conclusion. *Instead I start with an examination of two practices which are global in their reach and within which a very large proportion of humankind are already participating.*[56] These are the practice of global civil society and the practice of democratic and democratizing states. The argument of this book appeals to the self-understandings of those who are participants in these practices. The crucial point about these two practices is that both have the notion of individual human rights as a central component of their internal structure such that they cannot be understood at all without us having some understanding of the role of human rights within them. Similarly, because rights are so central to both practices, those of us (and we are many, worldwide) who are participants in them cannot but take rights seriously. A failure to do so would be an act of self-disqualification which would take us out of these practices within which we are constituted in ways which are ethically important to us.[57]

In the next chapter I shall make the case that the two global practices which I am discussing (which have notions of individual human rights as a central component of their internal structures) are both practices which are of particular ethical importance for us – for it is within them that we are constituted as free individuals.

3   Foundational practices

The reader might be prepared to go along with my argument to this point (that rights are a component of the two global practices in contemporary world politics which I have been discussing) and yet still wish to maintain that human rights are not all that important in that, although rights are an internal component of the practices in question, these practices themselves are not, all things considered, ethically very important for us (or alternatively that they are only important for some of us, a minority). In order to counter this suggestion I shall now make the case that these two practices are exceptional ones in that, for those of us who are participants in them, they are fundamentally constitutive of us as free individuals. There are two steps here. First, I shall show that we are constituted as rights holders within a specific kind of practice – instances of the type which Terry Nardin called 'authoritative practices' which are to be clearly distinguished from 'enterprise associations'. Second, I shall show that the authoritative practices I am discussing are of a special kind; they fall into that class of authoritative practice which have as a defining feature that they are *foundational*. It is the crucial role of rights within these that I wish to highlight.

Purposive associations and authoritative practices

Purposive associations (also known as enterprise associations) may be differentiated from authoritative practices (sometimes referred to as practical associations). In making this distinction I am building on a distinction drawn by Michael Oakeshott and subsequently taken up and developed for use in International Relations by Terry Nardin.[1] In what follows, I accept without amendment their portrayal of purposive association, but my understanding of authoritative practice is distinctly different from Oakeshott's original account and Nardin's subsequent elaboration of it.

Enterprises (or purposive associations) are associations in which people get together in order to pursue a common goal. For example, people might join Greenpeace with the specific aim of preventing the French government carrying out nuclear tests in the Pacific. Greenpeace, no doubt, has a complicated internal organizational structure which specifies who may become a member, how office bearers are elected, which committees are responsible for what campaigns, and so on. These need not concern us here. The key features of a purposive association are, first, that it is an association of people who are self-conscious about their shared purposes, and second, that from the point of view of the participants, the relationship between their association and their shared goal (in this example, the preventing of French nuclear tests) is an external one. If Greenpeace as an organization collapsed the people concerned could set up (or join) some other organization in order to pursue the same goal.[2] Multinational corporations (MNCs) present us with a further example of enterprise associations. MNCs are designed to pursue profit for their shareholders. If an MNC failed to deliver profits then shareholders would consider themselves justified in withdrawing their investment from the corporation in order to seek a more profitable investment with another MNC. From the point of view of the investors in question, such associations are merely instruments for the achievement of a goal (profit-seeking), which goal they have independently of any specific enterprise.

The purpose of an enterprise provides a criterion which both those in the association and those outside of it may use to evaluate the performance of the enterprise in question. For example, an international aid agency may be judged by its success or failure in raising funds and delivering aid. If it fails in its aims, both insiders and outsiders may plausibly launch an investigation to uncover the reasons for its failure and to suggest alternative ways of realizing these goals.[3]

Authoritative practices are quite different from purposive associations.[4] The defining feature of authoritative practices is that participation in them gives to the participants access to a whole range of values which are internal to the practice in question. Upon becoming a participant in an authoritative practice, an initiate gains a valued standing only achievable through his or her participation in such a practice. He or she also gains the ability to do certain things which are only 'doable' within such a practice, and gains the realization of certain satisfactions only to be had in that domain. In order to participate in such practices people have to learn the rules, roles, goals, traditions and ways of being which are *internal* to the practices in question. The following question acts as a test for distinguishing whether a social formation is an enterprise association or an authoritative practice. When asked 'What point and purpose is served by participation in this practice?', participants in an authoritative practice are likely to provide answers which are circular – answers of the form 'The point and purpose of participating in this practice is to participate in this practice' or 'I participate in this practice because it is the only way that I can achieve a value, which is very important to me, and the value in question is the one which I can only achieve through participating in this practice'. It is this circular dimension of answers to this question which identifies the practice as an authoritative practice. All this may seem somewhat obscure. Let me attempt to clarify the matter with reference to some examples. As is so often the case, the simplest examples are provided by those authoritative practices which we generally refer to as games.[5]

Consider the game of chess. We learn how to play chess by learning how the differently shaped pieces are set up on the board, how each piece is to be moved, how the game starts, what counts as a win, and so on. A novice who is inducted into the game acquires a menu of possible actions which he or she did not have before. Having learned the rules, a person is constituted as a chess player – a new standing for him or her. Note that it is misleading to think of the rules of the newly learned game as curtailing the actor's pre-existing freedom. Rather they should be seen as opening up a new set of possible actions for the actor who now has available to him or her that range of actions (that set of moves) which are only available to people who know how to play chess. Of course, knowing how to play a game (knowing the rules of the game) does not dictate precisely how any particular match ought to be played. How a person plays any particular game depends on, amongst other things, the player's ability, mood and temperament.

The crucial point in all this, though, is to note that the game of chess (like other authoritative practices) is a practice which is understandable in its own terms. Understanding the practice does not require of us knowledge of how it contributes to the achievement of some other purpose (or purposes) which could be defined independently of the game of chess itself. Specified individuals may, of course, take up chess for instrumental reasons: some to make money as professionals, some to pass the time (in jail, perhaps), some to find a common interest with their children (or with their aged parents), and so on.[6] But knowledge of such extraneous purposes is not a prerequisite for learning how to participate in the practice. I can learn to play chess without having any of these as my purpose for playing. No single external purpose unites all players of chess (or any other game). This is quite contrary to what is required for participation in a purposive association. If I wish to become the managing director of a purposive association, such as a corporation, for example, it is essential for me to know what the goals of that corporation are and to endeavour to advance these. Suppose the purpose of a particular MNC is to make automobiles and, through the sale of these, to make profits for shareholders. Although these are the goals of this particular MNC, these goals themselves are external to this or any other particular corporation. They are 'external' in the sense that I could have these as my goals prior to joining this corporation (or some other one) and they are goals which I could seek to achieve in any number of ways other than through becoming MD of this particular company (or any other particular company). The main point is that I could not sensibly become MD of such a corporation without knowing what these externally definable goals are.

How then do participants in an authoritative practice (in this case the game of chess) answer the question: 'What is chess for?' As I have already mentioned, it is a defining feature of authoritative practices that attempts to answer questions such as this one tend simply to 'peter out' or they become circular. In the end the participants are reduced to saying, 'This is how we (chess players, soccer players, netball players, athletes, etc.) do things and we do things this way because we wish to be chess players (soccer players, netball players, etc.).'

Suppose that as novices to the game we were to ask our instructor to justify some rule of the game. We might ask 'What justification is there for the rule which specifies the way in which a pawn may be moved?' The instructor may take us to be questioning whether the rule he or she taught us is indeed the correct one. To allay our doubts we might be referred to the official book of rules (or to a more experienced player) for confirmation of that rule. Alternatively, the instructor may take us to be asking a question about the history of chess – asking about the origins of the rule. We might then be referred to books on the history of the game. Suppose, though, that we persist with our line of questioning, asking 'What justification is there for limiting the way a pawn may move in the way the present rule does?' In pressing our question home, we might suggest that the rule disempowers the pawn vis-à-vis the other pieces on the board. We might propose amending the rule to achieve fairness between the pieces. Here the exasperated response is likely to be, 'This is how we do it in the game of chess, moving pawns in this way is a defining feature of the game. If you were to change the rule, it would become a different game – "Australian rules chess", perhaps.' There is an element of finality about this answer. The justification for the rule being as it is becomes circular – it becomes 'this rule of chess is as it is because it is a rule of chess'. The contrast with purposive associations could not be starker. In these, any rule will always be justified in terms of its contribution to the achievement of the externally defined purpose.

Of course, those within authoritative practices, such as games, may contemplate changing the rules of their practices. The rules are not set in stone. For example, in recent years the rules of cricket, rugby, soccer and tennis (and many other games) have been modified. Most existing games are modified versions of earlier forms of those games. Rugby, for example, is but a modification of soccer. What we need to note, though, is that the modification of authoritative practices is guided by criteria *internal* to the practice in question. If people no longer have the leisure to play and watch long, drawn-out, county cricket matches, cricketers might consider introducing a shortened competition, the so-called 'limited overs' match. In contemplating this change the criteria guiding their thinking will still be criteria internal to the game. What the cricketers will have to judge is how the rules of *cricket* may be changed to allow a shorter match. The overriding concern will be to preserve the character of the game.[7] This is in sharp contrast to what pertains when it comes to contemplating changes in purposive associations. Here the overriding concern is to achieve the goal in question. If this involves changing the nature of the association completely this does not matter. For example, when it comes to achieving the goal of supplying electricity to a region, a single transnational electricity utility might be proposed to replace five national utility companies. In this case no questions will be raised about maintaining the character of the utility. What matters here is the supply of electricity, not the character of the associations which supply it.

There are several things which we need to take note of here. First, an association might start out as an enterprise (purposive) association and subsequently become, for those participant in it, an authoritative practice. Consider the organization Amnesty International. From a certain point of view it is a purposive association designed to lobby for the release of political prisoners. Yet those participating in this association might, over time, come to value the organization, not merely for its instrumental role, but as an association within which they find themselves to have a certain standing (a standing as that kind of moral crusader to be found in Amnesty International). This might become a standing which they value for itself. They might consider it a standing which they could not have in any other way than through being an active member of Amnesty International. Where this happens an enterprise association has become (for some) an authoritative practice.

Second, an authoritative practice might be used (manipulated) by some participants for external purposes. This happens most dramatically when an activity becomes professionalized – when some people come to play a game for the external purpose of making money. But even where this happens it is still possible to understand and participate in the game without reference to this external aim of the professional players which is the making of profit through the playing of the game.[8]

Third, from the point of view of participants, expulsion from an authoritative practice is significantly different from expulsion from an enterprise association. Expulsion from an enterprise leaves an actor free to set up another association in order to pursue the same goal. Thus, for example, when South Africa during its apartheid era was expelled from its normal oil trading arrangements (which were clearly purposive arrangements) as a result of international sanctions against it, it simply sought alternative arrangements to secure the same purposes (the uninterrupted supply of oil). In sharp contrast, though, expulsion from an authoritative practice is quite different and possibly far more serious in its consequences for the actors in question. To be expelled from an authoritative practice has, for the expelled person, something of the character of *excommunication*. It involves one losing a valued standing in a practice and losing access to that range of valued activities which, by definition, could only be had within the practice in question. Expulsion here involves eviction from a form of life. This happens, for example, when one is suspended from participation in a game, expelled from a political movement, disowned by a family, excommunicated by a church, denied citizenship by a state, denied rights in a civil society, or when a 'state' is denied the right to participate in the community of states (as happened to Rhodesia after the white minority there made its Unilateral Declaration of Independence in 1965). To put the matter differently, expulsion or exclusion from a practical association results in the loss of a valued social identity. To lose an identity is something quite different from failing to achieve a goal. A soccer player's failing to make more money than some other professional player (a goal external to the game of soccer) is one thing, being excluded from playing the game at all (on grounds of cheating, gross misconduct, bringing the game into disrepute, and so on) is quite another, and its outcome is far more radical. The first kind of failure allows the actor involved to respond with a determination to try harder the next time around, whereas the second kind of failure disqualifies the person from any kind of participation in that practice.[9]

Fundamental authoritative practices

Although each of us is constituted as an actor in many authoritative practices, some of them are more important to us than the rest. The most important of these are those which are foundational for our sense of ourselves as valued human beings. These are those practices within which, through our participation in them, we are constituted as the actors whom we ourselves conceive of as having moral worth. In such practices we would judge exclusion from them to be damaging to our sense of ourselves as fully fledged ethical beings.

What practices are fundamental to us vary from one historical period to another and from one place to another. As an example of a very broad and inclusive authoritative practice which some of our ancestors considered foundational, but which many of us no longer do, consider the church in the Middle Ages. For most people in mediaeval Europe the church was a foundational authoritative practice which overarched many of the subsidiary practices within it. For them membership of the church was of fundamental importance and excommunication would have been considered an awful event, for it would have denied them the basic standing which they themselves thought necessary for human flourishing. For many people in the contemporary world the church is no longer such an authoritative practice. Its status has been eroded by the process of secularization. Part of my endeavour in this book is to determine whether that foundational practice has been replaced with another (or other) such practices.

Why is it important to elaborate this distinction between purposive associations and authoritative practices? And why is it important to make the further distinction between those authoritative practices which are foundational and those which are not?

The distinction between purposive associations and authoritative practices is an important one in that it highlights how very different the relationship between participant and practice is in each case. It highlights, that is, that purposive associations are merely *tools* for those involved in them. They are *means* which actors resort to in order to achieve the *ends* which they have independently of such associations. Thus when states sign agreements to co-operate in the domain of posts and telegraphs, or to co-operate in the development of transport links between one state and another, and so on, the associations formed as a result of such agreements are purely instrumental. The parties involved in such associations do not, through their association, create any common values between them which were not encapsulated in their pre-existing goals. Were the association to fail, the participants could resort to other means to achieve the same aims. Withdrawal from such associations may be calculated purely in terms of costs and benefits to the actors involved.

Authoritative practices are distinctively different. By participating in such practices participants create for one another values which could not be achieved in any other way. *Within such practices being a participant in the practice in question is itself the reason for participation.* The standings, values and satisfactions to be had in such practices as the practice of cricket, the practice of chess, the practice of

Christianity, Islam, Buddhism, and so on, can only be had by participating in them. The satisfactions of being a Christian, follower of Islam, Buddhist, cannot be had or even conceived of without participating in the Christian, Islamic or Buddhist practices.

The feature of foundational practices which makes them worth noting is that what they require from those who participate in them trumps the requirements of all other purposive and authoritative practices. Thus, for example, where actors from many different authoritative practices might come together to pursue a common purpose (as happens, for example, when Jews, Islamic people, Christians, Buddhists, Hindus and secular people join together in disaster relief efforts, or in campaigns to prevent the spread of AIDS) such joint action is only possible insofar as what is done does not infringe any of the constitutive rules of the foundational practices of the actors involved. Where a constitutive rule of the foundational practice applies this would always trump the rule of the purposive association and other lesser authoritative practices. Thus, a Jew could only act in such associations insofar is he or she was not required, in so doing, to infringe a constitutive rule of Judaic practice (and similarly for the other foundational practices).

What follows then is that any understanding of international relations (or any other realm of social relations) which confines itself to the level of purposive associations must necessarily be a superficial understanding, for it will not reveal the deeper constraints operative on the actors involved. It will not reveal those constraints which, from the point of view of the actors involved, override the requirements of purposive associations and other associations when there is a clash between the norms of the purposive association and those of the authoritative practice.

What makes foundational authoritative practices so important is that it is these practices which determine, from an ethical point of view, who the actors in question take themselves to be. These are identity-determining practices at the most basic level. It is these which determine for the actors in question what it is to be a person. Without knowledge of such practices we shall not know who people (including ourselves) take themselves to be and, a fortiori, we shall not be able to understand their past actions or anticipate what they might do in the future. In the final instance, it is foundational authoritative practices which determine the range of possible actions open to specific actors.

Let me recapitulate the core claims of my argument in this section:

- All of us participate in any number of practices.
- Some of these are purposive associations.
- Others are authoritative practices. The distinguishing feature of these is that they confer on us valued standings and create for us values which can only be had through our participation in such practices. These statuses and are internal to such practices.
- Some authoritative practices are foundational in that they create or consti-

tute us as actors with that standing which we take to be foundational to who we think we are as human beings.
- Where conflicts arise between what is required of us in one practice and what in another, the constraints of foundational practices trump those of all the other associations in which we participate

My claim in this monograph is that in our contemporary world, for those of us who claim individual rights for ourselves in both global civil society and in the society of democratic and democratizing states, these practices are both authoritative and ethically foundational. It is crucial that we understand this and that we understand the place of individual human rights in these practices because, for those of us who are involved in them, the constraints they impose will override any constraints which stem from our involvement in common purposive associations and in other less important authoritative practices.

These two foundational practices are fundamentally constitutive of who we take ourselves to be. In these two practices we are constituted respectively as civilians and citizens. The study of the core features of these practices and the evolving relationships between them I call constitutive theory.

In the next chapter I shall look in more detail at the role which notions of individual rights play in the constitution of these practices.

4 Individual rights in conflict?

Civilians versus citizens

A central contention of the argument so far is that in order to understand what we do in the domain of contemporary international relations, both individually and collectively, we need to understand the practices within which we are constituted as actors. A full understanding of these requires an understanding of the normative component embedded in them including the human rights component which is central to both.

In the previous chapter I explored the distinction between two different kinds of practices – purposive associations and authoritative practices. I made the claim that a subcategory of this latter group is particularly important for our analysis: this is the category of foundational practices. What makes this kind of practice so important for us (and for any other actor) is that it is in these that we are constituted as who we value ourselves to be. Were we not given the recognition we enjoy through our participation in these practices, we would consider ourselves to be fundamentally ethically deprived.[1] To understand who we are and what we do in the domain of the international, we need to investigate the structure of fundamental social practices within which we find ourselves to have the standing we value.

Constitutive theory is an approach which enables us to undertake an internal inquiry into the structure of foundational practices within which we are constituted. The analysis up to this point suggests that the questions which we have to ask ourselves are: 'Who do we value ourselves to be?' and 'In what set of foundational practices are we constituted as valued individuals?'[2] The answers to these questions would naturally lead on to further questions about the relationships which hold between the different foundational practices within which we are located.

It follows from the definition which I have given of a foundational practice (a practice which overrides or trumps the requirements of other practices in cases of conflict) that there must be coherence within the set of foundational practices within which we are constituted. For it is self-evident that we cannot simultaneously participate in foundational practices the requirements of which contradict one another. An example which forms a central focus of this book will make this clear. Suppose that I am constituted in the foundational practice of rights holders which we know as civil society. Being a foundational practice this requires of me that, where the rights-respecting requirements of this practice conflict with what is required of me in other social practices, the requirements of civil society will prevail.[3] But if I am at the same time a participant, as a citizen, in the society of democratic and democratizing states, which itself is a foundational practice, and if this requires of me that I flout the requirements of civil society, I shall then find myself in an impossible position. For if the requirements of the two practices contradict one another I shall not be able to abide by both. I shall face the question of the rights of which practice are to trump those of the other. In answering this I shall have to acknowledge that one of these practices is not really foundational for me. I shall have to acknowledge that my participation in one of them is not, at the end of the day, crucial to my standing as who I value myself to be, and that my participation in it is merely hypocritical.[4]

We are all constituted as who we value ourselves to be in a number of foundational practices. Insofar as they are foundational practices for us we have seen that it must be the case that these practices cohere. The interrelationship between such practices is often complex because the practices within which we are presently constituted did not arrive, as it were, ready made. They have a history. The constitutive practices of our time were preceded by a long line of different practices which constituted people as very different to us. For example, there is a great difference between those of us who take ourselves to be citizens in democracies and those people in the mediaeval period who understood themselves to be participants in an elaborate order of personal obligations. Some actor-constituting practices simply fell by the wayside with the passage of time – others remain with us. Often these have been modified. In many cases the old practices, suitably modified, have formed the basis on which new ones have been built. It often happens that with hindsight we can see just how the new practices have incorporated the old ones and have introduced new actor statuses which may be seen as improvements on the shortcomings of the earlier ones.

No theorist has given us a clearer picture of this kind of development than the philosopher G.W.F. Hegel. In his political philosophy, and in particular in his work *The Philosophy of Right*, he has presented us with a remarkable account of how we, as beings who understand ourselves to be individuals who are free and rational, are only constituted as such within a set of social practices with a remarkably complex history and which now fit together in an elaborate hierarchy.[5] The history which he traces is not the history of political, social and economic events, but is the history of that set of social forms which has led to the emergence of our being constituted as people who consider ourselves to be free individuals. He traces how components of our present self-conception of ourselves as free individuals were to be found in earlier social formations. But he points out how these only went some of the way to establishing us as free individuals because, in certain crucial respects, features of these practices actually impeded our emergence as free people. With hindsight we can see how these failures and contradictions, internal to a given practice, were overcome by subsequent social forms which subsumed the earlier ones and in so doing solved key contradictions within them. From our present point of view, we can see how, in turn, these subsequent social forms (within which actors were constituted as more free and rational than they had been in the earlier ones) once again displayed internal tensions and contradictions which were only overcome when further practices developed which subsumed the earlier forms, and so on. Hegel traced the whole process and in so doing outlined the architecture of the total set of practices which constituted us as the free people we take ourselves to be.

In answer to the question 'Who do we value ourselves to be?', the present monograph has, from the outset, addressed itself to those who answer this question with at least 'We are civilians (holders of the so-called negative liberties) and citizens (the holders of citizenship rights).' The practices within which we are constituted with these statuses are, I have argued, civil society and the society of democratic and democratizing states. If they are foundational practices, then, following the line of argument developed above, it must be the case that the two are compatible with one another and that they can both be shown to make a contribution to our being the people we value ourselves to be. If this cannot be shown, then we shall have to conclude that our participation in one of these practices is in some way fraudulent.

What I wish to do now is illustrate briefly, in a way that roughly follows Hegel's method, just how we are constituted as 'who we value ourselves to be' in a hierarchy of foundational practices. I shall start by considering the practices Hegel identified as central to the constitution of freedom. These are, as is well known, the family, civil society, the state and the system of states. This short overview will demonstrate how, starting with our current conception of ourselves as free individuals, we may with hindsight examine the hierarchy of practices within which we are established as such.[6]

In the family, we are constituted as actors of a certain kind. We are recognized as members of the family (father, mother, brother, sister, grandparent, cousin, uncle, aunt) each with a prescribed standing and a specified set of possible actions appropriate to his or her station. Typically within the family, members are required to love and respect one another. It is in the context of our families that most of us first come to be recognized as people who are of value and worthy of love within a social whole. Family membership is not something which we contract into for specific purposes. The family is not a purposive association. We do not decide to join a family. It is that social entity within which we, as children, first come to recognize ourselves as beings valued by others and to recognize others as setting store by our valuing them. Being a valued member of the family is our first experience of participation in an authoritative practice. There may well be argument about the strengths and weaknesses of different forms of family structure, about the merits of the nuclear family structure versus that of extended families or of traditional family systems. But there can be little doubt that this institution is the first within which we are constituted as beings who value one another insofar as members of a practice.[7]

From our present point of view, though, we can see that our freedom as individuals is not realized in the practice of the family. One problem is that participants in families see this social form as natural rather than as a social form created by people. We are inclined to see it as a given rather than a social construct of our own making. Another freedom-impairing aspect of the family is that in it members are accorded strictly prescribed roles – there is little room for individual autonomy. Furthermore, the idea of pursuing one's own interest is strictly circumscribed within the family. As a member of a family one is required to put the family's interests first. These shortcomings within the family are overcome when we move out of the family into other freedom-enhancing practices. As Bruce Ware interprets Hegel: The family 'remains incomplete in so far as it is incompatible with the full individuation of its members. The latter leads to the dissolution of the family as the children mature and set out to achieve their personal ambitions.'[8]

Once again, if we keep our present conception of ourselves as free persons in mind, we can see with hindsight how, as we grow up, we move beyond the family into civil society where we are constituted in a way which enhances our freedom. In this realm, some of the impediments to our development as free individuals which existed in the family are overcome. The improvement is brought about through our recognition of one another as the holders of certain basic rights. Civil society is the sphere in which individuals constitute one another as rights holders. In civil society we recognize one another as individuals who, on certain specified matters, may make decisions unconstrained by public policy and public opinion, guided only by our own chosen principles and interests. In it we are entitled to have interests which differ from other people's and we are entitled to pursue these, our own particular interests, subject to the constraint that we recognize the rights of others. In this sphere rights are trumps and, as such, they create areas of free choice which are proof against any override by the collective voice of others. Typical of the rights which we consider ourselves to have in civil society are the rights to security of the person, freedom of speech, assembly, movement, contract, conscience and the right to own property.[9] A major component of civil society includes what is known as the free market – that realm within which we recognize one another as beings who are entitled to own property and to buy and sell it. As Ware says 'On the surface, civil society appears as a realm of particularity, wherein individualism is given full expression and economic pursuits are paramount'.[10]

Civil society is a practice we enter into at a certain stage of our lives – we are not participants in it at birth. Initially, when we are very young, we are not considered to be fully fledged rights holders, but are treated as minors – as people with limited sets of rights. Later, when we have learned what it is to recognize rights in others and to claim them for ourselves (including what is involved in owning, buying and selling property), we are admitted to the practice of civil society.

Nowadays being a participant in civil society – being recognized as a rights holder – is fundamental to our sense of ourselves being fully fledged moral agents. In order to make this case, consider what our reaction would be were we deprived of this standing. At the limit, such deprivation would imply our enslavement. Suppose that far from allowing us to participate in civil society, others treated us as their private property – treated us as slaves. As such we would be denied the right to own anything, including our own bodies. Thus, a fortiori, we would not have the right to sell anything (either our things or our labour) and we would not have the right to make contracts of any kind. Were this to happen, we would consider it a serious setback to our conception of ourselves as who we are and who we value ourselves to be.

It is important to make the point here, once again, that it was not always like this. Not all people, everywhere, at all times have been constituted as rights holders. For most of recorded history there was no practice of individual human rights in the form of present-day civil society. For long stretches of history, in many places, property relations were communal. At other times, property in material things (and in people) was considered to be vested in the ruler (possibly a monarch). Then again, there were long periods of history when slave-owning societies were the norm. At such times the foundational practices constituted actors who had very different self-conceptions to the ones we have.

However, from our present perspective, we can see that civil society itself has freedom-impeding aspects. First, in civil society most participants do not have a conception of it as a social form at all. In particular, they do not understand it to be an authoritative practice within which they co-constitute one another as rights holders. For the most part they experience one another as rights holders warding off rights claims from others. They are not self-conscious about how within civil society they are engaged in a practice of mutual constitution. Second, far from members of civil society appreciating one another as co-constituters of their standings as rights holders, they experience one another as rivals in their respective pursuit of their own self-interest. Finally, instead of experiencing themselves as participating in a social whole within which all rights holders jointly establish one another as free actors, they often experience their participation as alienating.

Once again, having our present self-conception of ourselves as free individuals in mind, we can look back at our whole social context and see how being a member of civil society is foundational for us, but we can also see the limitations of that society as I pointed out in the previous paragraph. We can now see how many of these limitations have, in turn, been overcome in the social practice which we know as the state. Within the state we constitute one another as citizens, that is, as members of the polity with a very specific set of rights. In this form of mutual constitution, we recognize *both* the autonomy of each citizen, *and* the contribution each citizen makes to the whole state within which he or she is a citizen. In the state, we are self-conscious about our individual freedom as citizens and about how our individual freedom is granted to us by our fellow citizens through our joint participation in the state.

Finally, states do not exist in isolation from one another. The freedom we enjoy as citizens who co-constitute one another as members of a sovereign state would not amount to much were our state to become the victim of an imperial takeover. For our citizenship to count as establishing us as free individuals, we need to have our state recognized as autonomous by other autonomous states. The practice within which this takes place is the community of states, which must be understood as a fundamental authoritative practice. Sovereignty is a value internal to the international system of states. It can only be realized by states recognizing one another as they do in the authoritative practice known as the community of states.[11] Here again I wish to suggest that our being a member of this authoritative practice is fundamental to our current conceptions of who we value ourselves to be.[12]

It is important to point out that with regard to our constitution as the actors we value ourselves to be, it is crucial that we are participants in all these social practices. Thus were we confined to one of them, for example, the family, we would be less than free. In like manner, being a participant in only the family and civil society but not holding citizenship within the state would once again curtail our freedom.[13]

The authoritative practices which I have discussed above are fundamentally constitutive of our standing as free individuals. Membership of these practices is not something which we consider optional for ourselves or others. It is not something which may or may not be of instrumental use for the achievement of whatever other goals we happen to have. We consider membership of these to be constitutive of us as the individuals we take ourselves to be.

The constitution of freedom after Hegel

In the previous paragraphs I outlined the hierarchy of freedom-constituting practices following Hegel's rubric of family, civil society, state and interstate practice. This is somewhat misleading, though, for from the vantage point of the present, we can see that three of the practices he described have developed in dramatic ways since he wrote *The Philosophy of Right* and these developments have greatly extended the freedom which we enjoy.

In his work Hegel wrote of civil society as if it were coterminous with the state. He wrote of civil society that 'This system may be prima facie regarded as the external state, the state based on need, the state as the Understanding envisages it.'[14] Since then civil society has expanded beyond the borders of any particular state. We who regard ourselves as participants in civil society, as rights holders in it, do not consider that the corpus of rights holders ends at the border of our particular state. We consider all people to be rights holders whether they live in states or not. Furthermore, in the economic sphere, which Hegel saw as a major feature of civil society, this society has clearly extended to every corner of the world. In this domain, people claim rights for themselves, recognize them in others, and participate in the global marketplace pursuing their self-interest in a domain that stretches far beyond any particular state. Hegel wrote the following lines about civil society within the state, but it is now easy to see that what he wrote of then can now be taken as applicable to civil society worldwide:

> When men are thus dependent on one another and reciprocally related to one another in their work and the satisfaction of their needs, subjective self-seeking turns into a contribution to the satisfaction of the needs of everyone

else. That is to say, by a dialectical advance, subjective self-seeking turns into the mediation of the particular through the universal, with the result that each man in earning, producing, enjoying on his own account is *eo ipso* producing and earning for the enjoyment of everyone else.[15]

In what follows, in our account of our contemporary set of foundational practices, we shall have to take note of the greatly expanded scope of civil society – a society which has expanded far beyond its extent when Hegel described it – a society which may now properly be called global civil society.

A second major change which has taken place since Hegel wrote *The Philosophy of Right* is that many states have become democratic and, furthermore, the vast majority of those that are not democratic are committed to becoming so. It seems obvious to me that we have to construe this development as further progress in the realization of freedom. The establishment of democratic states advances the cause of freedom as understood by Hegel in that in democratic states citizens do not merely constitute one another with the valued status of citizen and, in so doing, constitute the state itself as a valued social whole. In democratic states citizens constitute one another as actors who may *on an ongoing basis* participate in the governance of the state which, as citizens acting together, they have constituted. There are, of course, ongoing debates among democrats about what the most democratic form of participation would be (I have in mind debates such as those about the merits of participatory democracy versus representative democracy, or those about the merits of different kinds of electoral systems), but it seems clear that citizens who constitute one another as beings who have a right to participate in their own self-government, through whatever democratic form, have a more developed form of freedom than that enjoyed by citizens in non-democratic forms of government. Our discussion of our present-day foundational practices will have to take note of the development of democratic states.

Finally, since Hegel wrote *The Philosophy of Right* the system of states itself has changed. There are now many more states, nearly all are committed to democracy, the vast bulk of existing states have voluntarily accepted membership of the UN with all of the normative commitments entailed in that, and they all freely participate in a system of international law that is much better developed than that which pertained in the early nineteenth century.

The changes in these foundational practices since Hegel have simply served to strengthen what I take to be the most important development in the progression from family to civil society, to state, and to the community of states, which is that at each step there is a more self-conscious articulation of the relationship between individual freedom and the social whole within which individuals are constituted as actors possessing such freedom. A crucial feature of the further elaboration of this process has been the centrality accorded in the higher order practices to the place of individual human rights.

Let us now take another look at the hierarchy of foundational practices with a view to showing how, as we move up the hierarchy, as each higher order practice subsumes the one below it and overcomes the freedom-impeding features embodied in it, rights come to play an increasingly important role.

Rights in the family

In the first of the fundamental ethical practices which I identified above, rights are only of marginal significance. In the family as we know it, parents have traditionally been considered to have a right to the obedience of their children and children to have a duty to obey their parents. In recent times, though, especially in the West, it has been said that children have rights, too. There is, indeed, an international convention on the *Rights of the Child*.[16] In many families children are regarded as rights holders. For example, in families with a liberal bent, children are granted the right to speak in the context of family discussions and the right to spend their savings as they think fit, and so on. These, though, are not rights properly so-called for they are held, as it were, on probation. They are granted to children by their parents and are conditional in that they might be withdrawn by the parents when and if the children abuse them. These 'rights' lack the trump-like aspect of fully fledged rights. Thus children might be granted the right to make contracts, but they do not have the right to sell their labour in full-time employment where this impedes their education. They are often granted a 'right' to freedom of speech, but this does not stretch to granting them a right to publish pornography. Their 'right' to freedom of movement does not stretch to a right to leave home at a tender age in order to travel the world. I could continue in this manner through the list of negative liberties. What we need to notice though is that children's rights are conditional; they are subject to parental veto. What protects children in the context of family life are the *duties* which parents owe their children. Although we might sometimes talk of children's rights to education, welfare, medical health, and so on, these 'rights' are best understood as duties owed by the parents to the children.[17] The 'rights' of children, which are entrenched in the positive law of many states and which are now a component of international law, are not rights in the full sense of the word, for they too cannot be waived by the children who are taken to have such rights.

Most importantly for my purposes, though, we need to notice that the notion of individual human rights is not central to the practice of family life in that it is quite possible to understand the workings of this practice without having any conception of individual human rights whatsoever. Insofar as the idea of rights does pertain to families, it is a watered-down, derivative concept of rights.

Rights in civil society

The place of individual rights within the context of civil society could not be more central. They are a defining feature of civil society itself.

In the argument thus far I have talked rather glibly of civil society. What precisely is it? Outside of the social sciences it is not a phrase in common usage.

It is not a term which those who are not social scientists often use or would easily recognize. We all know what a family is. Most of us belong to one and can easily identify our own family and those in which others are constituted. Similarly, the notion of a state is well known to us. We can all identify the state within which we live and can name at least some other states. But many people have never encountered the phrase 'civil society'. If asked which civil society they reside in, or, if asked where the borders of their civil society are, they would not know what to answer. Yet in spite of the unfamiliarity of the concept, I wish to maintain that many of us are members of civil society, that civil society is a society which can be conceived of as existing independently of the state and, very importantly, that our membership of it is fundamental to our ethical well-being. On the face of it, this claim of mine seems very odd indeed. How is it possible that people are not aware of their participation in a practice (civil society) which is fundamental to their standing as free human beings? Let me attempt an explanation of this conundrum.

Civil society is that society within which we recognize one another as holders of individual rights. We are able to detect the form of this society by paying attention to the way in which we talk and write about our basic rights and the rights of others.

Before proceeding with this task of detection it is important to recall that when we appeal to a right we are appealing to a reason for action (or inaction) which trumps other possible reasons for action. Thus an individual right can trump a collective preference, such as a majority decision by a legislature or even a group of legislatures across different states. Thus, within civil society, persons with a right to speak are recognized as having this right in spite of the fact that most of us (locally or globally) do not want to hear what they have to say; individuals have a right to associate even in those cases where most of us do not like the kind of association they are forming; property holders have a right to hold their property although a majority of us would prefer that it be confiscated and redistributed; and so on.

How is it possible that we are aware of ourselves as holders of fundamental rights, but are often not aware of the society within which we hold these rights? My answer to this is that we do not have a well-established concept of civil society because we do not generally consider our rights claims to indicate the existence of some kind of social practice. Furthermore, we do not experience our claim-making as taking place in a practice which is independent of the state. We fail to see it in this way, first, because the characteristic act of a member of civil society is, on the face of the matter, an act of disassociation; an act of the individual saying to the group 'No, I will and shall not co-operate because I have a right to do as I wish on this matter'. This is in sharp contrast to other social forms like families, churches and states. In these we consciously identify ourselves together with the other members of such families, churches and states as jointly forming the social practice in question – in each case this involves us in an awareness of an obvious solidarity with the other insiders of the practice in question. We who are members of such groups clearly identify ourselves as distinct from those who are outsiders to the group. We are aware of this solidarity even when we are engaged in acrimonious disputes within the families, churches and states to which we belong. In contrast, when we appeal to our basic rights, it seems, at first glance, as if our appeal is not one which we are making within the context of any social formation at all. It appears to be pre-social in some way. John Locke wrote of this domain within which we make rights claims as a state of nature.[18]

Second, our failure to think of our basic rights as being situated within a social practice arises from the way in which we often talk of these rights as *natural* rights. This suggests that we have such rights from birth simply by virtue of our humanity prior to our participation in any kind of society. The perception of the domain of rights as pre-social is conceptually wrong-headed. The activity of rights holding only makes sense within a social formation within which rights holding is a recognized form. Just as the idea of holding and playing a trump card only makes sense within the context of a specific card game. Indeed, far from a practice of rights being pre-social, it is a highly sophisticated social formation within which participants recognize rules which accommodate difference within a social whole. The society of rights holders encourages diversity to such an extent that participants may well lose sight of the fact that rights holding is a social activity within a specific social formation.[19] We tend to forget (or we simply fail to notice) that it is only within a highly elaborate social practice that rights can be held.[20]

Third, since we often pursue our rights by making use of the legal machinery within specific states, we may often be lulled into thinking that the context of rights is the context of the sovereign state with its associated legal system. What this line of thinking obscures from us is that making rights claims is not dependent on the existence or not of a state and a legal order. There is nothing nonsensical or incoherent about claiming rights in situations where no state or legal system exists.

I mentioned above that people do not have a ready answer to the questions 'To which civil society do you belong?' and 'Where are the borders of your civil society?' That we do not have answers to these questions is, I believe, particularly interesting in that it alerts us to some significant features of civil society. Paying attention to these features serves to elaborate yet further why we do not generally experience civil society as a social practice in the way that we experience families, churches and states as such.

The first feature I would draw attention to is that there are not *many* civil societies. There is but one. We are not locked into discrete civil societies in the way that we are members of discrete and identifiable families, churches and states. The realm within which we regard one another as rights holders is wider than the family (on gaining full majority we move out of the family into the wider world in which we stand as rights holders who may interact with other rights holders). It is also wider than the state, in that we consider those beyond the borders of our state to be rights holders too. I consider myself to be a holder of fundamental human rights and I thereby identify myself as a participant in the practice of civil society. As a rights holder, I respect valid rights claims by others wherever they happen to be – whether it be in South America, on islands in the Pacific, or in Africa. Because there is only one civil society and because it has no geographical borders, the participants in civil society lack any sense of belonging to some insider group clearly distinguishable from an outsider group or groups. Civil society lacks the inside/outside character which is such a defining feature of other groups.

A second feature to note is that we do not consider that the validity of the rights that people beyond the borders of our own state claim for themselves is in some way dependent on whether or not they are members of some or other state. Were the state in which they live to wither away, we would still consider them to possess their fundamental rights although, of course, we recognize that these might be difficult to enforce without the apparatus of the state. An immediate example is presented to us by the recent history of people in parts of what was the state of Yugoslavia. During the period of struggle in which it was not clear what states would replace the entity previously known as Yugoslavia, many people there did not live in a functioning state (with its associated legal system), yet, in spite of this, we clearly considered the people there to have their basic rights throughout the process. Much of the concern voiced by the United Nations and other international organizations rested upon the contention that human rights were in jeopardy in that region. The validity of rights claims by people in that area did not (and never does) depend on whether or not they live in functioning states. Another way of stating this is to say that claiming a right does not necessarily involve making a legal claim. Legal claims necessarily presuppose a legal system within which they are being made.

A third major feature of civil society is that it is an open society. Civil society, unlike the family, does not have a closed membership determined by blood ties, and, unlike the state, it does not have a closed membership linked in one way or another to a territorial location. Rights holders will accept into the fold of civil society any who claim rights for themselves and respect such rights in others. Anyone may join the society of rights holders by learning how to claim and how to respect rights. There are no formal entry procedures. There is no membership committee which vets applications and awards membership after full scrutiny of the applicants' credentials. Within this society there is no gate-keeping function with regard to new members and there is no prior procedure for deciding on the criteria to be applied by such gate-keepers. There are no criteria of exclusion such as race, class, age, ethnicity, gender, or sexual orientation. Joining civil society is not at all like joining a club, church or state, which almost always involves a three-step procedure that moves from application for membership to scrutiny of credentials, and culminates either in the closing of a contract of membership or in the rejection of such an application. In all such associations, the criterion (or criteria) for inclusion or exclusion is always an important topic. In sharp contrast to what pertains in such associations, this is never an important topic for civil society. A person who wishes to become an active participant in civil society merely has to learn how to claim rights for him or herself and respect them in others. One joins civil society in a way analogous to the way in which one joins the society of English speakers. One joins it by learning to speak and understand English. In like manner one joins civil society by learning to claim rights for oneself and to respect them in others.

Besides being open in this way, civil society is an open society in yet another noteworthy way. We need to notice its openness with regard to the treatment of people who are not actively participant in civil society – to outsiders. In terms of the rules of civil society, those who consider themselves to be the holders of basic human rights are bound to treat all adult human beings wherever they happen to be *as if they were already participants in the practice of rights holding.* Rights holders are bound to do this irrespective of whether the others in question understand themselves to be rights holders or not. In effect this indicates that civil society has a built-in open recruitment policy.[21] The doors of civil society stand open to everyone whether they live in a tribe whose people do not know what a rights holding society is or whether they live in a state (such as the former USSR or the present day Iraq) which is overtly antagonistic towards the participation of its citizens in the rights practice of civil society. The members of civil society, in other words, do not defend geographic borders or exclusionary criteria of one kind or another, but actively seek to open the society to all who would join it.[22] To treat someone *as if* they were a rights holder is not to coerce that person, but to offer a protected space for action which the person may use or not as he or she wishes. Thus to treat a woman living under conditions of extreme patriarchal domination as a rights holder is to offer her a chance to speak freely, to associate freely, to study, to move about freely, to own property, to make contracts, and so on. Of course, being treated as a rights holder does not require of the person thus treated that she should exercise all or any of the rights she is taken to have.

As illustration of this openness of civil society consider two examples, one hypothetical, the other taken from recent history. For the hypothetical example, imagine that we rights holders in civil society were confronted by a woman who presents herself as the owner of a slave whom she calls her husband. In gratitude for some service we have rendered to her she invites us to use or abuse her slave as we wish. The husband in this case understands himself to be a slave – an object owned by his wife (he has no concept of himself as a rights holder, but sees himself as a mere chattel). In this case, would we not, as rights holders in civil society, feel ourselves bound to treat him *as if* he were a rights holder in this society? We would be bound to act towards him in ways that granted to him the standard list of first generation rights. As members of civil society we would feel ourselves precluded from treating him as a mere thing; precluded from treating him as his wife does.

The example from recent history concerns the way in which rights holders worldwide responded to the white *baaskap* policies of the National Party government in South Africa during the apartheid era.[23] The rules of civil society did not allow rights holders elsewhere to agree to (accept, go along with, connive with, or participate in) *baaskap* over so-called 'natives' even if the South African government invited them to do so – as, indeed, it frequently did.[24] Participants in the practice of rights holding elsewhere were obligated to treat South African blacks *as if* they were already participant in the practice of rights holders. Many of them, of course, already were participants in civil society and demonstrated this through their use of the language of rights.

That all people are to be treated as if they were rights holders has the effect of obscuring from rights holders that their rights holding takes place within a social practice, within civil society. The link between holding rights and participating in civil society is obscured from us by the language used by participants in civil society. People in civil society typically say: 'All human beings have basic rights'. This statement seems to be an assertion about the way things are in the world whether or not the humans in question are part of civil society. What the statement seems to suggest is that people have such rights whether or not they belong to this, that or the next kind of society. Rights it appears are what individuals have independent of their societal memberships. But this statement, 'All human beings have basic rights', needs to be understood from within the practice of civil society. Seen from within the practice this statement in fact elides two different assertions: The first being that 'We in civil society regard all participants as having an equal set of basic rights'. The second is 'We in the practice are committed to treating those outside of it *as if* they were already participants claiming basic rights for themselves'.[25]

A fourth feature of civil society may be stated as follows: civil society can exist (and persist) even where the participants lack the means of enforcing their rights. Thus, although rights holders in civil society may use various means to implement and enforce their rights and although the most important mechanism of rights enforcement is likely to be the state (through the mechanism of a judiciary and a police system), it is important to notice that we consider civil society (the society of first generation rights holders) to be conceptually distinct from these mechanisms. It is distinct in that we can well imagine civil society existing without states.[26] This is a point made several times already, but it is worth repeating. There are many areas of the world (especially in Africa) where 'states' are not functional – where the 'states' have become what are now often referred to as 'quasi states'.[27] Where this has happened (and when it happens again, as no doubt it will) rights holders elsewhere still maintain that people in these areas are to be recognized as rights holders. They are not to be considered rightsless simply because they lack the means to enforce their rights. Similarly, in circumstances where states have collapsed (as happened in the USSR), members of civil society elsewhere persisted in their belief that the people in that area were still holders of basic human rights. Were some (or all) of the states in which we rights holders presently live to collapse, we would still claim that we had fundamental human rights. In seeking to defend these under such circumstances we might well resort to the use of non-state instruments of enforcement. For example, we might do this through the use of private enforcement agencies. This kind of rights enforcement is already taking place in Africa. In cities with less than fully functional states, citizens have resorted to private rights enforce-

ment agencies to protect themselves. In many places, corporations have subcon-
tracted protection out to private enterprise, and, indeed, in some cases the
governments of quasi-states have called in the services of private enforcement
agencies.[28] The central point, though, is not to discuss the justifiability or merits
of these enforcement agencies, but to indicate that in the absence of the state to
enforce our rights, we (like the rights holders in these areas) would not cease
thinking of ourselves as rights holders, and we might well think of making use of
mechanisms other than the state to protect our rights.

A fifth remarkable feature of civil society is that it is a society without any
central authority; it is a society without government. Rights holders in one place
recognize the rights of others wherever they are, whether or not they fall under
some common government. I recognize the rights claimed by others whether
they be in Somalia, Swaziland, Switzerland, or on the high seas – that we have
no common government over us is neither here nor there with regard to our
respecting one another's rights. Since civil society, as such, has no government, it
has no corporate policies on any matter whatsoever. It has no policies on infla-
tion targets, immigration quotas, anti-pollution measures, or deep-sea
fishing-catch limits. Within civil society there is no legislature and there is no
debate about appropriate legislative programmes. An implication of this is that
within civil society there can be no party political activity directed at gaining
control of the society, for it is not a society with a unitary identity which is available to be controlled. There is no seat of power to be won in a power struggle.
Crucially, within civil society, because there is no legislature and no legislative
programme, there is no 'high politics' about the distribution and redistribution of
revenues raised from public taxes. Of course, rights holders within civil society
might argue with one another about who should get what. They might do this
within the contexts of the other associations to which they belong, such as families, churches and states. But these questions do not arise for civil society as a
whole, for the kind of whole it forms is not the kind for which such questions can
arise. An implication of all that has been said above is that there are some issues
in civil society which have been taken, as it were, completely out of politics. In
particular, the basic rights themselves which constitute civil society cannot
become the subject of political bargaining within civil society conceived of as a
polity. This is so because it is not a polity. In this society, rights holders understand their rights to be independent of any particular overarching authority.
This has implications for how change comes about in such a practice. By definition it cannot come about through a process of central decision-making or
through a process of constitutional change. Instead it will always come about in
an incremental and indirect way.

Sixth, because civil society has no geographical borders and no government,
it has no security policy. There are no borders to police and there is no national
security council to consider how the borders and core interests of civil society
ought to be defended. When it comes to security, civil society is best thought of
as being akin to the World Wide Web. The web was designed to be proof against
a certain form of attack. It was designed to have no heartland the destruction of

which would knock out the whole system. The ideal was to construct a system such that whatever small or large bit of it was destroyed, the rest could continue functioning. Of course, the ideal was somewhat constrained by the vulnerability of certain nodes in the 'hard-wiring' of the world. Civil society is similarly indestructible; furthermore, unlike the web, it does not have the vulnerable nodes which the web has. There is no government of civil society which could concede defeat of the whole. Civil society will continue to exist for as long as there are people who continue to recognize one another's rights. This form of reciprocal recognition can be done publicly or clandestinely; it can be done over wide areas involving many people, or amongst small pockets of people. This kind of recognition may be given to others under the very noses of authoritarian or totalitarian regimes.[29] Civil society can exist in a contiguous whole, or in dispersed pockets.

To recapitulate: the primary feature of civil society is that it is a practice of first-generation rights holders. Within civil society people are not slaves, serfs or subjects but individual rights holders. The bundle of rights which each individual is taken to possess grants to him or her an area within which he or she can take his or her decisions independently of the wishes of others. From a rights holder I may confidently buy that which is his or hers to sell. I say 'confidently' for if she has the title then by definition she is the one who may decide whether to sell or not. No further parties need to be involved in the decision. With a rights holder I might confidently form an association to advance the purposes we both have. I have no need to refer beyond him or her (to a father, for example). It might happen, of course, that a state or some other interfering party might attempt to hinder my deal with the rights holder, but from the perspective of civil society we would judge such a state to have done wrong; it would have overstepped the bounds of what states and other associations are permitted to do.

All this may be summed up by saying that within the fundamental practice of civil society, through claiming rights for themselves, people constitute one another as individuals, each with a specific area of protected autonomy. In civil society I may choose when, to whom and about what I may speak. In civil society I may choose with whom and for what purposes I shall associate. In civil society it is for me to decide which god I shall worship and how I shall do it. In civil society I may choose which books to read (and so on, through the set of individual rights). Interference with these rights of mine – whether by individuals, gangs, or governments – is wrongful interference.

Rights in the practice of democratic and democratizing states

In the previous section we saw how rights are a central component of that fundamental authoritative practice which we call civil society. I showed how it is not possible to grasp the concept of civil society without an understanding of the notion of individual right. In like manner an understanding of *a different set of individual rights* is central to gaining an understanding of the fundamental authoritative practice of the democratic state, which itself is but a component of the practice of democratic and democratizing states. In this foundational practice a new set of rights comes into being, and through the creation of a new kind of rights holder, the citizen, some of the problems encountered in civil society are overcome.[30] Baldly put, we cannot even vaguely understand what a democratic state is without having some ideas about the individual rights involved in democratic citizenship. To put the matter differently, these rights, the rights of the citizen, are constitutive of the practice of democratic states. Understanding democracy requires an understanding of the place played by these rights in the democratic practice.

In all democratic states citizens have a set of rights associated with citizenship. This extended set of citizenship rights includes a set of rights enabling citizens to participate in the election of government.[31] There are rights granting citizens the right to stand for election to government. There are rights which enable citizens to hold the government to account during its term of office. These include rights with regard to freedom of the press, freedom of information, freedom to form lobbies to put pressure on government and freedom to form political parties which can recruit candidates to stand for election, co-ordinate policy positions across issue areas, round up the vote at times of elections, and keep elected members of government in line with party political positions.[32] These democratic rights are rights which are defined in terms of a constitution which may be written or unwritten – formal or informal.

As citizens, people have a right to be treated equally within certain spheres of activity. Thus, for example, as a voter each citizen has a right that his or her vote be given the same value as those of other citizens. Each has a right to insist that the government of the day, in making its policy, will take into account his or her interest and that it will not govern only in the interests of, for example, men as opposed to women, blacks as opposed to whites (and so on). Furthermore, citizens have a right (a claim which may not be trumped) that their democratically elected government govern the state in their interests and not in the interests of the members of neighbouring states. Citizens have a right that their government protect their interests from dangers which emerge both within the territory of their state and from beyond it. As part of this, they have a right to carry a passport and a right, while they are abroad, to have their interests protected by the diplomatic service of their state.

I could go through the details of citizenship rights in much greater detail, but the central point is now clear. The idea of the citizen as a rights holder is fundamental to our understanding of the practice of the modern democratic state. No sense could be made of a democratic state without some concept of the democratic rights of citizens. These are rights which may not be taken from citizens. A government which deprived citizens of such rights would no longer be a democratic government, but would have become an elitist, autocratic or totalitarian government. The general point about the centrality of rights to *any* understanding of a democratic state applies whether one is speaking about representative democracy, participatory forms of democracy, republican forms, or other 'mixed' forms of democratic polity. The fierce rivalry found in debates between proponents of different understandings of democracy in no way defeats the general point that a defining feature of democracy is that it is a form of polity within which citizens have certain specified rights in key processes of government.

It is crucial to note that the rights which we hold within a democratic state are rights which are fundamental to our standing as the free individuals which we take ourselves to be. The democratic state and the rights which citizens hold within such a state are not merely instrumental to the achievement of some goal or goals which we, the participants in that state, might happen to have. The rights of citizenship are important in their own right not merely as a means to some end. Were we to be deprived of our rights as citizens we would deem ourselves to have been deprived of something of great moral worth. One indication of this is that around the world there are liberation movements which assiduously seek to have such rights granted to them. Another is that one of the world's largest lobbies ever (the Anti Apartheid Movement) campaigned successfully for just these rights for the disenfranchised in South Africa during the apartheid era. The basic argument underlying this campaign was that depriving the majority of people in South Africa of citizenship rights was depriving them of a fundamental ethical status. This is not to deny, of course, that citizens normally hope to make use of their rights to bring material benefits to themselves, such as the provision of education, healthcare, housing, and so on. But to point only to the instrumental value of being a voter does not catch the full meaning we attach to this status.

Another point worth noting is that having the rights of a citizen in a democracy is not only important to those commonly called 'liberals'. It is a central component of the thinking of nationalist movements as well. Where national groups (however defined) engage in liberation struggles for national self-determination, a central component of their ultimate goal is the establishment of a democracy within which the members of the movement will have the democratic rights vis-à-vis their government which I have described above. In the current context of world politics, nationalist movements do not seek to establish absolute monarchies, dictatorships, autocracies, or totalitarian orders. They seek the establishment of democratic states within which the members of the nation will be free to govern themselves.[33]

I have outlined the key role of one set of rights within civil society and another set of rights within the democratic state, and I have indicated how depriving participants in these practices of their rights would deprive them of something fundamental to their sense of who they are and who they value themselves to be. But the democratic state is but a component of the wider practice of democratic and democratizing states, which itself is a foundational practice for those who participate in it. This is the foundational practice within which democratic and democratizing states recognize one another as sovereign. Another way of putting this is to say that it is a practice within which each state recognizes the right of other democratic states, and the citizens which comprise them, to autonomy within a certain domain. For example, within the society of democratic states the people and government of the United Kingdom recognize the right of the people and government of the USA to manage their domestic affairs as they think fit (but subject to certain constraints discussed below) and vice versa. Note that in this practice individuals constitute one another indirectly. We have seen how individuals first constituted one another as rights holders within civil society, and then, second, how they constituted themselves as political rights holders within the democratic state. Now at this higher level citizens within democratic states, through their governments, recognize the sovereignty of other democratic states and by so doing they validate the autonomy of the citizens in those other states. In return they have their autonomy validated by them. By recognizing the autonomy of other democracies, citizens in one democracy confirm the citizenship rights of people in other democracies, and confirm their right to be self-governing in their area. A sovereign democratic state has a right with which it can rebut even the majority decisions of other states (such as a majority decision, for example, to carve up the target state into a set of colonies to be distributed among the majority).

It is also important to realize that the rights of states and the rights of citizens are co-constitutive. When the citizens of a state such as Britain recognize the right of autonomy of the USA, they are recognizing the rights of all US citizens to mutually constitute one another as such and by so doing to constitute the USA as an autonomous state. The individuals in the USA, in turn, by recognizing the sovereignty of Britain, recognize the individual rights of people in Britain to constitute one another as citizens in that autonomous state. Were the USA to deny Britain such recognition and to pursue a policy aimed at colonizing her, the citizens in the USA would be denying to the British people their status as citizens in a sovereign democratic state which is fundamental to their status as free individuals in this broad foundational practice.

In the practice of democratic and democratizing states, there is nothing sacrosanct about any existing set of states within which people constitute one another as holders of citizenship rights. What matters is that people are constituted as citizens in *some* set of democratic states that recognize one another as such.

It may be contended that what I have said above applies to democratic states, but that the majority of the states today are not democratic. Their right to autonomy thus cannot be derived from the rights of the individuals who comprise the state in question. In response, I would remark that even those states which are not currently fully fledged democracies with regular open and free elections are accorded sovereignty on the grounds that this will enable the people there to create a democracy in due course. The members of the practice of democratic and democratizing states do not simply accord sovereignty to states in order that the government of the day in the sovereign states may rule in whatever way they wish. It is expected of them that they will move their states towards fully fledged democracy. Proof of this is to be found in the rhetoric of the participants in the practice.[34]

Summary

In this chapter I have argued that, as things presently stand, we, the people, who consider ourselves holders of first generation rights, and who consider ourselves entitled to enjoy citizenship rights in democratic states, are constituted as such through our being participants in the following practices: civil society and the international society of democratic and democratizing states. These are not purposive associations through which we seek to realize values that we have independently of these associations, but are practices within which we realize, through our participation in them, certain values that could not be realized in any other way. Furthermore, these practices, I have argued, are foundational in that our being constituted as participants within them is of fundamental importance to our self-conception of what it is to be free individuals. Finally, and most importantly for my present purposes, I have shown that central to both of these fundamental authoritative practices are rules which confer on the participants in them individual rights with which they can trump collective arguments that may be put forward by other participants in these practices. Rights-conferring rules are at the very heart of the practices discussed in that, were the rights-conferring aspect of the practices to be eradicated, the practices would no longer be what they presently are and would have become something altogether different. A fortiori, the actors constituted within those practices would have become actors of a different kind.

5   Civil society

The space for global politics

I have argued that I, myself, and many others worldwide have this in common: we are constituted as free persons through our participation in two authoritative practices which are global in their reach. These are civil society (the society of first generation rights holders) and the society of democratic and democratizing states. Sets of individual human rights are a central feature of both practices.

These practices are authoritative practices as distinct from purposive associations. Their defining feature is that through our participation in them we both constitute one another as having a certain kind of valued standing and we realize certain values amongst ourselves. This standing and these values are not to be had in any other way than through our participation in these two practices. For it is a defining feature of authoritative practices that participation in them can be understood as an end in itself, not as a means to some other externally defined end.

I argued in Chapter 4 that the two global practices in question are not merely authoritative practices, but they are, for those of us who participate in them, foundational too. Were we to be denied participation in them, we would consider ourselves to have been fundamentally ethically damaged. Thus we would consider ourselves to have been ethically harmed were we no longer accorded the status of rights holders in civil society. In like manner, it would be a major ethical setback to be denied the standing of citizen in the practice of democratic states. This would involve, amongst other things, not being granted the status of a person with moral standing enough to participate in the election and the holding to account of the governments under which we live. To be denied these things would be to reduce us to servitude of one kind or another – an ethically devastating outcome.

In this chapter I shall explore more fully the major features of the first of these ethically foundational authoritative practices, civil society.[1] Global civil society has many quite extraordinary features which are seldom noted. In particular, in what follows, I shall be drawing attention to the way in which global civil society can be understood as the framework which makes possible a certain form of civil politics at both the local and global levels. In this chapter I shall focus on the positive features of civil society. In the following chapter I shall discuss the very considerable negative aspects of civil society and then discuss how some of these are remedied in the society of democratic and democratizing states.

The general description of civil society with which I have been working is that it is a society of first generation rights holders. It is a society which has only recently achieved global reach. Civil society comprises all those many men and women worldwide who, like me, consider themselves to be bearers of first generation rights and who recognize others as having such rights. This practice consists of those who know how to use the language of rights. It consists of the people who participate in the global conversation about individual rights.

In what follows, after a short digression to respond to some critics, I shall proceed to a more fine-grained analysis of civil society.

On using constitutive theory: a response to some critics

When presenting the ideas contained in this book to various forums, I have often encountered the following criticisms: Why haven't you engaged with the extensive literature on global civil society and globalization?

My response to this criticism is that I am engaged in normative theory and not in sociology. Let me elaborate. Much of the debate about civil society in the literature referred to by the critics, is directed to describing what civil society is, explaining how it came into being, and/or explaining its effects on the contemporary global social order. A good example of this kind of sociology is to be found in Justin Rosenberg's *The Empire of Civil Society* in which he challenges the dominant realist approach in IR, according to which the system of sovereign states is to be understood as the driving force of contemporary international relations.[2] In opposition to the realist paradigm, Rosenberg argues that we can only understand the modern state once we have understood how it emerged from an expanding global capitalist system. He argues that the set of social relations found in civil society effectively drained away certain political functions from the public–political realm, where they had previously resided, to the private domain of economic transactions between rights holders. For Rosenberg, civil society is currently the dominant global social structure. In the sociological debate about civil society there are many who challenge this position. Realists argue that the structure of power between states is dominant in the international realm and that civil societies exist within states and are constrained by them. Liberal institutionalists argue that civil society is a social formation which may be envisaged as standing between the powerful realms of interstate relations, on the one hand, and the behemoth of global capitalist relations, on the other.[3] There are many other permutations to the sociological literature.

In this book I am not concerned to enter this sociological debate, although I fully acknowledge its importance. This debate is, of course, central for those engaged in the business of social explanation.[4] Clearly, for sociologists, it is important to describe what civil society is, to explain how it came into existence, to explain what structural power it exerts over states (individually and as a set), to determine whether there are forces within global civil society that, in the long run, might undermine the existence of the system of sovereign states, and so on. A recurring question in the sociological inquiry has been: Is the global capitalist system a threat to the Westphalian order?

In tackling these kinds of questions sociologists have to engage with the whole gamut of problems encountered under the broad rubric of social scientific method. These have to do with the collection and measurement of data, theory building, the influence of theories on what are taken to be the facts, questions to do with verifiability (and/or falsifiability), model building, and so on. At a deeper theoretical level they also have to do with the epistemologies and ontologies with which the sociologists operate.

This monograph is not to be understood as a contribution to sociology insofar as it is taken to be a discipline focused on explanation. It is also not to be understood as contributing to the sociology of ideas which is the bread-and-butter business of post-structural and post-modern theories. Thus, I am not concerned to take on the very interesting task of explaining the mechanisms, techniques, movements, double movements, processes of exclusion and inclusion, hidden processes, and so on, which are used to construct the subjectivities of those who participate in civil society or in sovereign states. Furthermore, I am not engaged in uncovering the mechanisms which produce different subject positions and identities.

My task is a different one. It is to focus on that which is prior to any attempt at social explanation. The prior requirement is that before we, as would-be social scientists, can start producing explanations, we must have some understanding of the actions to be explained, whether they be our own or the acts of others. For example, it is not possible for me or anybody else to seek explanations for certain patterns of voting behaviour before we understand what it is for someone to be constituted as a voter amongst other voters – before I know what is involved in voting. In like manner, it is not possible for me (and others) to seek explanations for instances of gross human rights abuse (such as a genocidal event) before we understand what actions constitute such an abuse. Again, we cannot begin to explain why interventions by states into the domestic affairs of other states take place under some circumstances and not under others, before we understand what constitutes an intervention by one sovereign state in the internal affairs of another. All the social phenomena that sociologists seek to explain depend on a prior characterization of the phenomena in question as being instances of a certain kind of human action. In order to make such a characterization the acts have to be understood. Doing this requires an involvement with normative theory. It is this engagement which I am both demonstrating and exploring in this work.

In this book I am, at every point, both addressing and seeking to understand those, who, like me, make certain claims for themselves. In particular, I am interested in our claim that we have certain fundamental human rights (the ones which I am specially interested in are the negative liberties) and in our claim that we have certain rights of democratic citizenship. I take the group of people who make such claims to be very large indeed. In this book I make the case that these rights claims we make only make sense in the context of certain social practices. It is the details of these practices which I seek to explore. What can we, who make such claims for ourselves, say about the practices within which these rights claims are located? What can we say about the relationships which hold between the practices and what can we say about the normative commitments embedded in them? *This is an inquiry into the internal features of the practices within which we make these rights claims. It is, one might say, an investigation of the logic of the language we rights holders use about ourselves.*

Our inquiry in this book is similar in kind to the inquiries which we can imagine being undertaken by people in the following hypothetical predicaments:

1   Imagine a group of people who claim themselves Jews and who at the same time claim themselves citizens of a newly established communist state. For them the following questions might become questions of fundamental importance. What is it to be a Jew? What would be involved in being at one and the same time, a Jew, a communist and a citizen in this new state? Is it possible to reconcile these statuses? Clearly, for these people there is scope for great debates about what is, or ought to be, involved in being simultaneously a Jew, a communist and a citizen? These debates will not be primarily sociological, but normative. The parties to this inquiry are not likely to commission a sociologist to answer such questions for them. They are not likely to issue a sociologist (who might be realist, structuralist, post-structuralist, critical or post-modern in orientation) with the brief: (a) determine what is involved in being Jewish, in being communist, and in being a citizen, and then (b) establish whether these are complementary identities. The kind of data-gathering and theory-building for the purposes of explanation which is at the very heart of 'doing sociology' for sociologists of all ilks, is not appropriate to actors facing this kind of question.[5]

2   Imagine a group of people who consider themselves committed members of both the global community of scientists, on the one hand, and committed members of the global free market, on the other. This group comes to confront the issue of intellectual property rights as it pertains to some new discovery (the Human Genome Project, for example). The question which presses upon them is that as members of the community of scientists they are committed to the free flow of ideas, whereas as members of the free market they are committed to the institution of private property which includes the right to own ideas. What ought they to make of this tension? Here again it seems clear that the question is not one which it would be appropriate to hand on to sociologists for resolution. The answer which they are looking for is not going to be found in theories which explain the history of modern science as we know it. Nor is it to be found in theories about the long and complex history which led to the establishment of what we now know as the global free market. These explanatory theories, while inter-

esting, are not appropriate to the solution of the normative problems which face these actors.

When we, as actors, find ourselves in the kind of predicament which I have sketched above, we are faced with questions about who we are. The answer we give to such questions will then determine how we should act. What we require here are not explanations, but complex normative interpretations, which interpretations require of us that we take normative theory seriously.

To recapitulate, my answer to those who query my failure to engage with the sociological literature on civil society and globalization is that I am not engaged in a sociological inquiry, but in a normative one. I am not seeking to explain how the rights-holding practice came into being, or what the likely effects of its existence are going to be. Instead, I am attempting to elaborate the internal logic of the global practices within which we, who claim individual rights for ourselves, are constituted as people who make such claims. This is an exercise in constitutive theory.

When we are engaged in constitutive theory we are called upon to evaluate one another's arguments in a very specific way. For example, in this chapter on global civil society I shall be making certain assertions about prominent features of this society. When I do this I wish to be understood as saying to those who, like me, claim first generation rights for themselves: 'Is it not an implication of the claims we make for ourselves that the practice within which we make these claims has the following features?' This is an invitation to all those who claim rights for themselves to engage in a set of thought experiments in which they try out the claims which I have made and compare them with various other possibilities which might come to mind. They are invited to consider whether the rights claims which we make for ourselves are, or are not, compatible with the features of the practice which I have proposed. If not, then what alternative propositions about the practice would do the trick? The assertions which I make in this chapter about the main characteristics of the practice within which we make rights claims are not descriptions of states of affairs, but are claims about what is implied by what we say and do. The reader is invited, as a participant in these practices, to test my claims against his or her own self-understanding of the practices in question.

Let me now press on with a detailed analysis of some of the features of the global civil society – the society within which we recognize one another as the holders of certain fundamental first generation rights.

On the relationship between claiming rights and being able to enforce them

The rules, conventions and norms of civil society, the society whose existence is entailed in the rights claims we make, do not prescribe what means rights holders should use to protect their rights. Instead, we understand that the rights we claim to have within civil society place constraints on what instruments we may adopt to enforce our rights. These constraints allow for the adoption of a wide variety of different enforcement mechanisms. Let me elaborate.

Individuals who participate in this discourse of rights, which I call 'civil society', differ greatly in their capacity to enforce their rights. Some of us may live in states which are well equipped to protect our rights, while others, who do not live in such states might, nevertheless, possess sufficient means to set up private protection associations to safeguard their rights.[6] Some who live in weak states might turn to international organizations such as the UN, Human Rights Watch, churches, and many other organizations of one kind or another, to help them enforce their rights; some might set up political movements to do this, while others, who find access to such organizations difficult, might be reduced to using whatever means of self-help they have to hand (these may be more or less successful). That different people turn to different means to enforce their rights should not hide from us that in their possession of rights we take all these people (with widely different abilities to enforce their rights) to be equal participants in civil society. Whether one is a participant in civil society or not depends on whether one claims rights for oneself and on whether one recognizes them in others, not on what instruments of enforcement one has to hand. All the different means of enforcing rights are legitimate provided that the means used do not themselves contravene the rights of civilians.

The most important point to note here is that from the point of view of civilians the state is not the only legitimate means of enforcing his or her rights. Under certain circumstances private enforcement agencies might do the job as well, or even better. If states fail to enforce rights adequately civilians may justifiably turn to private agencies to do this for them. This is a phenomenon which has become prevalent in many parts of Africa at the moment, and in terms of the argument which I have presented, there is nothing ethically repugnant about this course of action.

Civil society: global and open

The language we civilians use in civil society implies that it is a global society in two ways which need to be distinguished clearly.

First, we understand it to be global in that those who participate in it, those who claim for themselves first generation rights, may be geographically spread out (although not necessarily evenly) and are not confined within territorially defined state-like jurisdictions. We accept people into civil society (accept them as participants in the practice of rights claiming) no matter where they happen to be. They may be located on any continent. Some live in highly developed states while others live in weak, collapsed or quasi states. Some live in democracies, others in authoritarian states of one kind or another. Some are settled in one place, whilst others are migrants.

Second, it is global in that participants in this practice are committed to treating all sane adult people wherever they happen to be *as if* they were participants in civil society. They are committed to treating those who are not active in civil society and who have no conception of themselves as rights holders *as if* they were fully fledged self-conscious participants in it. This commitment of rights holders to treating others 'as if' they, too, were active in the rights holding practice is often expressed in ways that lead to great confusion. The confusion arises from rights holders making statements such as 'all people have basic human rights' or 'human rights are universal'. These statements seem to suggest that people have these rights whether they think and act as rights holders or not. What makes these statements problematic is the patent existence in the world of some people who do not speak the language of basic liberal rights and of people who vehemently reject human rights discourse.

The precise difficulty here can be brought out most clearly when considering the case of people who overtly reject the suggestion that they possess human rights. Such people are to be found in certain religious orders, for example. When civilians insist, in the face of such denials, that such people be treated as rights holders, this insistence may, on the face of the matter, seem pernicious in that it suggests that such people have rights in spite of the fact that they deny this. This stance may be interpreted as suggesting that such people are 'intellectually challenged', 'rationally underdeveloped,' or 'primitive' in some way for failing to comprehend the rights which they have. On this interpretation, the assertion of civilians that rights be applied universally appears, at the very least, to be highhanded.

However, I wish to argue that the conclusion of this line of reasoning – the conclusion that claims about the universality of human rights are morally arrogant – rests on a misinterpretation of what is being claimed here. There is an alternative interpretation of these assertions (that human rights are universal) which does not indicate arrogance but its opposite.

The assertion that all people have human rights, that they are universal, I suggest is quite plausibly understood as shorthand for the following.

First, it may be read as a shorthand statement of the membership criteria of civil society. It indicates that this society will accept all comers – it will not exclude would-be participants on grounds of race, class, gender, sexual preference, nationality, ethnic origin, religious affiliation, intellectual ability, educational qualification, conviviality, or whatever. It specifies that this is an open society. If someone wishes to participate in it, he or she may do so.

Second, it (the universality assertion) may be read as referring to an internal injunction within civil society which specifies how participants ought to treat non-participants – about how to treat outsiders. The injunction is that 'outsiders' are be treated *as if* they were 'insiders'.[7] This interpretation does not have the negative implications which normally attach themselves to assertions about the existence of 'universal human rights'. On the interpretation which I am offering, being committed to treating non-participants in civil society 'as if' they were rights holders cannot be read as implying that such people are challenged in reason, backward, primitive, pre-modern, and so on. If I, as a practising rights holder, treat you as one too, although you do not understand yourself to be currently a participant in civil society, my action towards you is not arrogant but is better construed as indicating a *commitment* from me to you, rather than as indicating a judgement by me about your limited access to the powers of reason. An analogy might be useful here. When a family decides to treat a stranger as a 'member of the family' this is quite rightly usually understood as a gesture of hospitality and generosity which is extended by the family to the beneficiary, rather than as a negative judgement upon the stranger's powers of reason. In like manner, the universality rule in civil society may be understood as requiring civilians to offer membership and participation to outsiders rather than understood as the making of a negative judgement about them. That all people shall be treated as rights holders is, one might then say, the hospitality requirement built into the internal structure of civil society.

Insiders and outsiders

In order to put some flesh on my suggestion that the universalist claims made within civil society may best be interpreted as an invitation to those who are not participants in it, rather than as an arrogant judgement on their core ethical beliefs, let us consider possible courses of action open to rights holders when confronted by non-participants – people, that is, who do not currently act or think of themselves as rights holders.[8] As mentioned above, typically, such people are to be found within certain religious practices which are hostile to the very idea of human rights because it grants individuals a measure of sovereignty over their own lives rather than portraying them as subject to the sovereignty of God. In order to reduce the relationship to its simplest components let us say that in such cases *civilians* (members of global civil society actively participating in the human rights practice) face *non-participants*.[9] It seems to me that we civilians understand the rules of civil society to exclude the following options:

1 They rule out a campaign to eradicate, conquer or subject the non-participants through the use of force. In order to understand why we civilians would reject this, we need to remember that for us to enjoy the standing of free people we need to be recognized as such by others. If we set out to conquer the non-participants we would be casting them as the enemy. They in turn would cast us as their enemy. They certainly would not view us as free people, but would see us as oppressors. The more force we used, the more likely it would be that the non-participants would forever regard us as conquerors. When we, who are participants in civil society, confront those who are not members of our society, by opting to conquer them, this rules out (or makes highly unlikely) the possibility of establishing, at a later date, an ethical relationship between us – a relationship within which we could constitute one another as free people through mutual recognition of one another as rights holders.[10]

2 We might consider simply containing the non-participants by keeping them at bay. From the point of view of military strategy, this might be an astute thing to do. But with a view to establishing our standing as free people vis-à-

vis the non-participants this would not be a viable option. Suppose for example that we civilians established a well-policed border behind an elec-trified fence.[11] Unless the non-participants recognized the fence as a boundary marking the extent of our authority, they would no doubt see the fence as blocking their access to resources, blocking their movement, and blocking a whole range of other possible relationships which might have developed between them and us but for the border. For example, they might see it as blocking the possible formation of friendships, affairs of the heart, sporting relationships, and so on. The non-participants might well see the border as an imposition by us upon them. A relationship between an imposer and those being imposed upon is not a relationship which civilians would actively seek out, because the ethical drive of civilians is to be recog-nised as people who legitimately hold certain basic rights, not as people who impose them upon others. In short, civilians seek to be recognized as free people by free people.

3   We civilians might consider simply ignoring the non-participants. At the extreme this would involve ignoring what they do (and have done), what they say (and have said), how they are (and have been), what they make (and have made). If we rights holders chose to ignore the non-participants, from their point of view this would probably be considered hostile, disrespectful, uncaring, or cruel (or all of these). It is certain that they would not recognize us as the holders of a set of basic liberties. Indeed, they might retaliate by ignoring us, in which case we would deem ourselves slighted, insulted (and so on), since (by definition in this case) they would not be acknowledging and respecting our basic rights.

The three options discussed above are ruled out from the point of view of civil-ians because accepting any of them would set up a relationship with the non-participants which would allow them to see us as overlords, imperialists, or simply as 'the enemy'. Instead, we civilians seek to be recognized as free people (as the holders of equal sets of basic liberties) by people who understand them-selves to be free in just this way. Pursuing the options mentioned above (conquest, subjugation, containment, and the ignoring of the 'other') would not create the conditions of possibility for this form of recognition and could not result in the establishment of a relationship of mutual recognition in which the free recognize the free. This, then, raises the question: What kind of action should civilians use vis-à-vis those who overtly reject human rights discourse (however small this category might be)?

The problem we are confronting is: What is it ethical for us civilians to do in our interactions with those who overtly oppose human rights? We need to find ways of responding which leave open the possibility of an ethical relationship emerging between us. In particular, it requires finding a way of relating which does not immediately turn our relationship into a master–slave relationship (this being a general way of stating the weakness of the three options discussed above) and which leaves open the possibility of a mutual relationship of ethical recognition developing. At this point it is worthwhile exploring, if only briefly, three recent responses to this question, none of which, I shall argue, is ultimately satisfactory.[12]

A first response is that put forward by post-structuralist theorists. Examples of these in the discipline of International Relations are Michael Ashley, William Connolly and Rob Walker. These authors would recommend to civilians that they adopt an approach to themselves and to those outside civil society which radically questions fixed identities and fixed boundaries.[13] They would recommend refusing to privilege any partisan point of view. What is called for, in their view, is an ongoing questioning of our own subjectivity and that of others. This general approach, an approach 'in the register of freedom', is designed to avoid privileging one particular ethicality (*Sttlichkeit*) at the expense of the ethicalities of others. David Campbell, informed by the work of Levinas, follows a similar line. He seeks to avoid a view which gives pride of place to our own ethical conceptions in a way which demeans the ethical conceptions of others. He argues for an ethic of responsibility towards otherness.[14] This involves a stance of permanent critique towards all totalizing discourses and the adoption of an ethic which positively appreciates the value of otherness.

A second approach to consider here is that adopted by critical theorists in International Relations who have taken their lead from Jürgen Habermas.[15] In their view, when the proponents of any ethical position confront those holding an alternative point of view, the question of the validity of their respective ethical positions arises. Critical theorists typically put forward discourse ethics as a means for testing the validity of the competing positions in such circumstances – as a means for settling such disputes. Discourse ethics recommends doing this by subjecting rival ethical positions to open and uncoerced discussion.[16] Those principles which achieve uncoerced consent at the end of this process are valid. What is required then, from the point of view of critical theory, is an inclusive realm within which such unconstrained dialogue can take place. This procedure would lead, if it were applied successfully, to consent on a universally applicable ethical system.

The third approach which I wish to mention is the one put forward by H. G. Gadamer and recently applied to the context of International Relations by Richard Shapcott.[17] Gadamer suggests that where we confront rival ethical positions we ought to engage in conversation with the other party(ies). In such a conversation both our own perspective on ethics, and those of the others involved, will come under scrutiny and a reciprocal educative process will take place. In this process, a blurring of the horizons of the parties to the conversation will occur and between them a new ethical point of view will arise.

I have sketched, in a way that does them scant justice, the conclusions of three complex and elegant approaches to the problem of the ethical standing of outsiders. There are major points of disagreement between these approaches which I cannot go into now. However, I believe that the summaries I have given are sufficient for my present purposes. These three approaches to the problem of 'the other' are, in many ways, similar. At first glance they seem highly attractive.

They are similar in their insights about the character of social scientific inquiry and their insights about the relationship between social scientific inquiry and ethics. They are also similar in what they recommend with regard to ethical inquiry. With regard to the character of social science, they are all historicist; they stress that our ethical codes and the ways in which we put them into practice are the products of a long human history. Our practices, they insist, are not 'natural' and 'given' for all time, but are the results of power struggles down the centuries. This insight applies to ethical practices too. Thus, our present set of social practices with its built-in normative position is but one of many possible ones, past, present and future. Each is now, or will continue to be in future, the product of its time. None is natural.

The three approaches recommend similar ways of dealing with the ethical puzzles which arise in a plural world – they recommend solutions which turn on conversation, questioning and dialogue, rather than on the justified use of force. In many ways, the three approaches under consideration are highly attractive to readers from liberal democratic traditions, for they appear to be open, tolerant, accommodating of diversity, modest, humble, not arrogant, and opposed to imperialism of any kind. But there is, I believe, a weakness in these approaches which stems from an unexamined point of departure in all their arguments. *The kind of questioning, conversation and dialogue which they advocate all presuppose a prior unacknowledged commitment to the norms and values inherent in civil society as I have portrayed it.* The questioning, conversation and dialogue all presuppose that we who are about to engage in such questioning, dialogue and conversation with non-participants are committed to behaving as good civilians from civil society. This presupposition is not spelled out in these theories.

In order to make my point let me get back to constitutive theory. In this section I have been presenting a confrontation between we who consider ourselves civilians and those who reject the rights on which civility is based. We civilians are looking for an ethical relationship with those who are not active participants in civil society. For us civilians this means achieving a relationship that is not based on a master–servant relationship (either of us over them or them over us). What is sought is an uncoerced relationship. This is sought because a coerced relationship could not result in the system of mutual recognition we seek. It was this consideration which prompted us to reject the options discussed above (conquest, containment, or the ignoring of the other). As far as we are concerned, an arrangement within which we and those who are not civilians can come to an ethical recognition of one another as free beings can only come about through dialogue and conversation. This would seem to align us with the post-structuralists, critical theorists and Gadamerian conversationalists under discussion. *What distinguishes the approach of constitutive theory from these, though, is the recognition that constitutive theory would not accept all forms of questioning, conversation and dialogue as ethical. For constitutive theorists the only ethical form of questioning, conversation and dialogue is that which takes place within a socially constituted framework with certain very specific features – a framework with the characteristics of a civil society as I have sketched it.* Conversation is an activity that is only possible within a social arrangement within which the participants adhere to certain rules. These rules determine who may be admitted to the conversation, what standing must given to the participants and what procedures are to be followed once the conversation is started.

Consider the first of these: Who is to be admitted to the conversation? Suppose we entered into conversation with a leader of a social formation (tribe, nation, religious group,) who sought to prevent others in his group joining the conversation on the ground that tribal, national or religious lore/law did not allow it.[18] Would we (should we) as rights holders accept this? I think not. For were we to agree to this limitation on who may join the conversation we might inadvertently be contributing to the maintenance of the subjection of women, blacks, Christians, Jews, Muslims, etc. We would be in the dark about an important counter-factual. The crucial thing we would not know is whether a conversation with the parties thus excluded might not have revealed that they, the excluded ones, found the existing structures of authority within their society thoroughly oppressive. For this reason we, as rights holders, would insist on treating all individuals *as if* they were participants in civil society and, as such, had the rights necessary to participate in the conversation of humankind. For example, we would insist that all individuals have a right to freedom of speech. Treating individuals in this way, of course, leaves open the possibility that the wives, blacks, Albanians, Palestinians, Muslims, and so on, who were to have been excluded from the conversation by their leaders (usually male) might in the end, after having joined the conversation, come to endorse the stance taken by their (usually male) leaders. Wives might profess their happiness at the subservience demanded of them within marriage, blacks might accept that whites ought to speak for them, Albanians might admit to taking pleasure in Serbian dominance, the Islamic laity might accept that it is proper to be subservient to Mullahs, and so on.

What I am suggesting then is that when rights holders (civilians) encounter those who are not participant in civil society, they, as rights holders, are committed to eschewing policies aimed at conquering, containing or ignoring such people, for these would block the possibility of the emergence of an ethical relationship with them. The achievement of an ethical relationship depends on the parties reaching agreement. We civilians are committed to achieving this through means which embody the values we are trying to realize. For this reason we shall choose as our means of negotiation, uncoerced conversation/dialogue with them. From the point of view of rights holders, this kind of conversation requires treating the others *as if* they were rights holders.[19] Doing this opens up the possibility for dialogue which is subject only to limited constraints. From the point of view of we who are rights holders, the very notion of dialogue and conversation requires of us that we treat such people in this way. Our idea of conversation and dialogue (as opposed to the issuing of commands and the holding of monologues) presupposes that we shall restrain our conduct in certain ways. We constrain ourselves by treating the others as having a right to freedom of speech (even though the others might not consider themselves to have such this right). Conversely, in order for the conversation to take place we shall insist on the right to free speech for ourselves. For, if the others deny this to us, then whatever communication took place between us would not be conversation or dialogue but monologue.

The institutional requirements of conversation and dialogue extend far beyond the requirement of free speech. For civilians and others to meet to discuss their differences requires that both accord one another the rights usually grouped under the rubric 'rights of the person'. The most important of these include the right not to be killed or assaulted. No unconstrained conversation is possible without these. Also, the participants must be granted the right to freedom of movement so that they might make contact with one another in order to exchange ideas about the construction of mutually acceptable practices between them. Rights holders may not connive with, for example, authorities (which may be the governments of states, the patriarchs of families, or the leaders of churches) who take steps to prevent those under their authority joining the dialogue about ethical differences by confining them within the border of the relevant state, homestead or parish. For a rights holder to connive in this would involve being party to excluding such people from the ethical discussion. In order to achieve this condition of conversation the rights holders will treat the subjects of such authority as if they were participants in civil society, as if they were civilians with the right to freedom of movement. Thus, when the Myanmar government seeks to exclude Aung San Suu Kyi from the discussions about the political future of her country, civilians everywhere are bound to object – are bound to reject the rationalizations which the government of Myanmar might produce for its actions.

Similarly, in order to secure the conversation which is required by civilians seeking to establish ethical relations with others, the participants will have to be treated as having freedom of conscience (also known as religious freedom). Rights holders will treat the other parties to such conversations as if they had a right to hold to whatever religious creed they wished. Thus, civilians confronting those in Africa and elsewhere who dispute the individualistic human rights codes to which many 'Western' people subscribe are committed to granting such disputants the right to hold (and to bring to the conversation) religious convictions completely at odds with their own. A failure to do this would amount to the exclusion of particular voices from the conversation.

Other components of the conversation which need to be established are: the participants need academic freedom in order to consult amongst themselves and to delve into the literature about the ethical questions which arise in the course of the conversation. Thus, rights holders will regard it as important that they and others in the conversation have open access to the academic resources which have accumulated over the years with regard to the specific ethical issues which might come up for consideration. Civilians will thus object to authorities that seek to limit the access of their followers to the ethical ideas of, for example, Jesus, Mahomet, Locke, Marx, Rawls, Buber or Levinas.

In like vein, a free conversation will depend on the participants having freedom of assembly (to discuss the issues with others), and a free press (through which to disseminate core ideas to others and have them tested in public debate).

In summary, then, the questioning, conversation and dialogue recommended by the theorists I have been discussing seem to require, as a starting point, participation in and a commitment to something like civil society as I have sketched it.

Recruiting civilians

Treating non-participants *as if* they were participants may be understood as a particular way of recruiting outsiders into civil society. It is a remarkable recruitment procedure with several different features which we need to examine more closely.

The path to recruitment into civil society is opened when active participants in the practice, civilians, treat non-participants as if they were rights holders. This is done in the hope that the non-participants will come to appreciate the standing thus conferred upon them and will in time become active civilians themselves. The recruitment process here is diametrically opposed to methods which rely on the use of force (the press gang), to methods which rely on a 'hard sell' advertising pitch followed by a formal membership drive (a method often used by evangelistic churches), and to methods which rely on the deliberate deployment of social power (as happens when those who control key resources make membership of a certain political party a precondition for accessing resources such as welfare, housing, loans, and so on).

Who does the recruiting in civil society? It may be done by the individual rights holders (individual civilians) or by groups of them acting in concert. Civil society as a whole has no central authority with a recruitment policy and has no administrative apparatus dedicated to that task. Each individual rights holder is a recruiter insofar as he or she obeys the injunction to treat both fellow participants and non-participants as rights holders. Thus when I treat migrants (who may be legal or not in terms of the positive law of some state) as possessors of basic human rights, even though they have no conception of themselves as rights holders, I am acting as a recruiting agent for civil society. I am setting up one side of what, with time, I hope will become a reciprocal relationship of mutual recognition.

Although the basic recruitment agents in civil society are individual civilians, it may well happen that groups of them will form associations for the advancement of human rights. They may set out to propagate the underlying philosophy of the rights practice formally in the hope that people exposed to such campaigns will soon start claiming human rights for themselves. Organizations such as Human Rights Watch do this. Larger, more comprehensive, human associations such as the state and international organizations might also set out to promote participation in a human rights practice.[20]

Who are the targets of recruitment? This question somehow misses the mark because, from the point of view of civilians, everybody is to be treated as a rights holder whether or not they conceive of themselves as such. It is not the case that some are singled out for recruitment and others are not. The language of civil society does not allow for civilians to distinguish between a chosen group, who are to be treated in one way, in contradistinction to those not chosen, who are to be treated differently. Because no distinction is drawn by civilians between insiders and outsiders, civilians do not need any overt recruitment policy towards non-participants. It almost seems as if the idea of recruitment does not make any sense here, for if civilians are committed to treating everyone as a rights holder, there is, from their point of view, no outsider group to be recruited! How are we to make sense of this puzzle?

It cannot be denied that treating those who do not actively consider themselves rights holders *as if* they were already civilians is a form of recruitment process. But this is a form of recruitment which is so different from the normal forms of recruitment that the term hardly seems appropriate in this context. In the normal case, when I am trying to recruit someone to join, let us say, the local institute of international affairs, I do this by presenting him or her with a list of good reasons for joining – such as 'being a member will increase your understanding of international affairs', 'being a member presents you with a chance to meet a wide range of experts in the field', and so on. My aim is to convince the person to undertake the act of joining. The benefits which I offer are withheld until the person joins. The recruitment procedure which relies on treating non-participants as if they were rights holders is strikingly different. Here I do not offer reasons for joining and I do not offer a package of benefits which are withheld until the requisite contract is closed. Instead, from the outset I confer upon the non-participant the benefits of participation in civil society, I confer upon him or her all the recognitions appropriate to a rights holder. The benefits are not made conditional on joining. The onus now falls on the recipient to argue why I should not recognize him or her as having a full set of rights, but should accept that she is a chattel of her husband, he a slave to white man, she a minion to some master, and so on.[21] This recruitment procedure puts the onus on the non-participants to produce arguments as to why they do not wish to be deemed to have a set of rights equal to the sets of rights held by civilians. It is up to them to justify why they should be at the bottom end of an unequal relationship; why they should not be treated as the holders of a set of basic liberties equal to the set held by everyone else.

Who, then, are the 'outsiders' who are possible 'targets' for recruitment in this somewhat back-to-front procedure?[22] They are those people who are not actively and self-consciously participants in civil society. Such people might be found within various social formations that reject human rights. These might include families, tribes, ethnic groups, religious orders, political parties, or states.[23] Although the targets for recruitment might be found within such social formations, and although it is the targets' membership of such formations which is or has been the bar to their participation in civil society, the recruitment effort is not directed in the first place against the social whole (family, tribe, ethnic group, religious order, or state) in which the targets live, but is directed at the individual people within those social practices. The recruitment effort is not directed to *defeating* these social entities. It does not involve any formal confrontation between an insider group (civil society) confronting an outsider group (the clan, the nation, the religion, etc.) The recruiter for civil society is not in a hostile relationship to an 'other' who has to be brought around to the rights way of thinking. When I, as a rights holder, write about the traditional tribal woman whose basic rights are being denied her by her husband, I do not cast her as the enemy that has to be brought around to my way of right thinking. From my point of view, it is not a matter of finding a way of defeating the family, tribe, religious order, or state within which rights are denied her. What I seek to do is have her claim basic rights for herself against all social formations which would deny them to her, including her own present tribal one. By acting towards her as if she were a rights holder, by speaking the language of rights to her, I hope to woo her into speaking the language of rights too. The recruitment campaign is not a belligerent one. Civil society does not endorse crusades based on force. For force cannot bring about the kind of society which civil society is.

An implication which flows from the fact that in civil society the primary recruiters and the primary targets for recruitment are individuals is that the recruitment process does not have to wait for the formation of policy by public authorities, or for concerted action by parties, churches, trades unions, states, etc. Rights holders engage in recruitment (through treating others as rights holders) at any time, with any individuals, at any place where they are able to make contact with such individuals. Recruitment is not subject to the constraints of any higher authority and does not involve the prior amassing of social, political or military support. It simply depends on what individual rights holders say and do. Thus, for example, rights holders in Britain advance the conversation on human rights worldwide by writing, talking, teaching, film-making, faxing, phoning, emailing, taking pictures, etc. All or any of these methods help make others aware that we regard them as having rights which they might claim for themselves. All these actions indicate that were they to do so (were they to claim rights for themselves), we would recognize the legitimacy of their claims. Even a conversation amongst friends about the abuse of rights taking place in Rwanda, for example, is a contribution to the recruitment efforts of civil society. For such conversations contribute to public opinion which indirectly provides support for campaigns for human rights in Rwanda and other distant places.

Beyond inside/outside

An intriguing aspect of civil society is that participation in it is not an all or nothing affair. The contrast with other kinds of social formations is quite striking. One either is or is not a citizen of a state, a member of a family, a communicant in a church, a player in a game, a member of a political party (communist, socialist, liberal, liberal democratic, nationalist, etc.). In all these cases where the members of one organization seek to recruit members from another organization, there comes a point where the targets of such a campaign have to decide where they stand – they have to have an answer to the question: 'Are you one of us, are you in or out?' Often joining one association involves leaving another. A person might leave one state in order to become a citizen of another, leave one political party to join another, convert from Catholicism to Protestantism, and so on. Using parliamentary jargon, we might say that the target has to make a decision to 'cross the floor'. This is a determinate act, and often a public one too.

Becoming a participant in civil society is quite different; here one may learn to speak the language of rights gradually and one may step by step come to claim individual rights for oneself. In this process there is no overt moment of joining civil society, the rights practice. No moment at which it might be said that one is leaving, deserting or betraying another practice. There is no moment of conversion. There are several points to be made here.

First, an important feature of civil society is that an individual may become participant in it incrementally, clandestinely, partially, jokingly, unobtrusively, inconspicuously, in a parodic manner, tentatively, and so on. It might happen like this:

> A woman in a traditional society (living under the Taliban in Afghanistan or under traditional Zulu rule in South Africa, for example) hears discussions about human rights on the radio. It occurs to her that she would like to claim such rights for herself. She starts to measure her life against the template of such rights language. Using this language, secretly at first, she talks to her friends and corresponds with individuals, groups from outside the traditional order, pointing out to them how her rights, and those of other women similarly placed, are being abused. In this way she gradually becomes a participant in civil society.
>
> Later she uses rights language in something of a joking way in her family setting, saying to her husband, 'I have my rights, you know' (followed by a laugh to indicate that this is merely light-hearted banter, nothing too serious). In this way she introduces the language of rights to her family – even in the face of hostility. After this, she might actively start claiming rights for herself in discrete corners of her life – when she participates in the marketplace, when she is amongst like-minded women friends, when she participates in the activities of other participants in civil society, such as aid workers, UN personnel, academics, teachers, and so on. In all this, there is no single point at which the patriarch within the family can say that his wife has definitively abandoned the traditional order and joined civil society. For she has no membership card, her name appears on no list, there has been no induction ceremony to incorporate her into civil society, and there has been no emotional conversion moment before some public congregation. What has happened in this sketch, is simply that she has learned the language of individual human rights and has begun in an incremental manner to apply this language to the circumstances of her own life.

In the fullness of time, no doubt, contradictions will emerge between the norms which govern her actions within civil society and the norms governing her actions within the traditional patriarchal order. But there is no stark moment of transfer from the old order into civil society. A consequence of this is that it is almost impossible for the traditional order to police its borders for deserters, turncoats and heretics who have turned to the discourse of human rights. Individuals may start participating in civil society while at the same time continuing their participation in the traditional social orders.

A second important feature of civil society to mention here is that the relationship between participants and non-participants is not well portrayed with the *friend/enemy* distinction. Many encounters in the history of the world between insider groups and outsider groups of one kind or another have led directly to military conflict. The histories of the great empires fit this model, as do the religious wars of the Middle Ages. In like fashion the great conflicts this century between fascist and non-fascist social orders and between liberal democratic states and communist ones – all of these were conflicts between defined friends and enemies.[24] In all these cases, the antagonists understood themselves to be defending a particular ethical order against some rival order. In sharp contrast the relationship between rights holders active in global civil society and those people who are not participant in it is not well portrayed as a relationship of enmity. For those in civil society are committed to treating non-participants as rights holders – treating them as participants not as enemies. Furthermore, as we saw in the previous paragraph, civil society presents no clear border, physical or abstract, between those who participate in it and those who do not. This is so since in civil society participation is not an 'all or nothing' affair. A member of a traditional tribal system in Africa, for example, can be simultaneously active in the traditional system and, at the same time, participate in civil society by, perhaps, being active in the local sphere of the global market. Such a person cannot be portrayed as friend or foe by either the traditional order or by civil society. The friend–foe distinction, if indeed it exists at all in such cases, exists within the mind of the individual herself insofar as she feels an antagonism between her identity as a civilian and her identity as a tribeswoman.

In the light of the above, we can see that for those millions of people who are partially active in both civil society and in traditional non-rights-based societies, no clear battle lines can be drawn between the two societies.[25] Insofar as the relationship between civil society and traditional societies is of concern in world politics (and it must be of great concern given the scale of global civil society), this relationship has to be analysed in terms other than those of traditional IR, which portrays conflicts, alliances, balances of power, and so on, as being between clearly demarcated groups. Civil society is not a discrete society which confronts other societies in the way that one nation might square off against another, one state confront another, and so on. Instead civil society threads its way through other social formations. Thus it is that civil society is able to expand rapidly into traditional social orders without setting up an overt conflict between clearly discernible groups. It can, and often does, expand without dramatic confrontations, campaigns or battles.

Global civil society then is a foundational authoritative practice which is so constituted that it can expand and woo new participants without any direct confrontation with other social forms.

Civil society and 'the other': transformation not domination

What I have said above may be restated slightly differently. To become a participant in the rights practice (in civil society) is not to become a participant in a practice which is exclusive. Participating in it does not require that one should leave one foundational practice (the family, the tribe, the nation, the church, the state) in order to join another (civil society). What happens as one becomes a participant in civil society is that one acquires a widely recognized language with which one can challenge aspects of the internal arrangements of other practices within which one is a recognized participant. People who challenge patriarchy from the point of view of civil society are not engaged in waging a crusade against the family form as such, but are engaged in a campaign to reform it so that it moves from being a patriarchy to becoming something less authoritarian. In like fashion, the newly participant rights holder (the new civilian) who challenges the traditional structure of tribal authority is not seeking to destroy the family, tribe, nation, church, or state. In each case, what happens is that as they become participants in civil society, this involves them in a project to reform these other social institutions in ways that will acknowledge them as holders of basic human rights. In sum, then, joining civil society does not require or entail anything so drastic as divorce, detribalization, rejection of the nation, or immigration. Civilians seek transformation not victory.

Civil society: a framework for politics

A major characteristic of civil society is that it creates a space within which participants and non-participants alike can engage in a certain kind of politics – a politics prior to the *polis*, a politics before the state. The basic freedoms which civilians accord to one another and to non-participants, too, gives to everyone a protected space from which they may critically discuss the social institutions within which they live. It provides them with a space from within which they can consider alternative social and political arrangements. The kinds of social arrangements which may come up for discussion include social units such as families, firms, churches, states and international organizations. From the point of view of civil society, no social arrangements, including civil society itself, are off limits for discussion within the forum created by this society.

Civil society creates the possibility for politics understood as a certain kind of activity. It creates space for politics understood as critical conversation between people about the basic rules of association which hold between them. This is politics as it was understood by, amongst others, Aristotle, Bernard Crick and Michael Oakeshott.[26] This view of politics, I believe, accords quite closely with our ordinary language use of the term. We often reserve our use of the term 'politics' for those occasions on which people who are participant in some practice turn to discussing (often disputing) the basic rules of association within that practice. Thus, within the family in day-to-day life we do not say that everything which takes place is politics, but when patriarchy becomes an issue and women seek to change the basic authority structure, we would recognize this as an exercise in politics – it is politics in that it involves a challenge to the basic rules of that association. In like fashion, the normal functioning of a firm is for the most part apolitical, but when the issue is raised about worker participation in management, this we regard as company politics. Much day-to-day administration within states may be considered apolitical, but when decisions about the laws of the land are to be made (whether in the realm of ordinary legislation or with regard to constitutional issues) then politics takes place. Similarly, in the international realm much day-to-day interaction (trade, communication, sporting contact, tourism, etc.) is apolitical, but when the 'underdeveloped' states seek to establish a new international economic order, this must be seen as an attempt to have the basic rules of association changed, and may thus be seen as an exercise of politics.

Politics as defined above (discussion about the basic rules of association), I wish to suggest, must be distinguished from the exercise of naked power or force. This way of making the distinction between acts which are political and acts of power (or force) once again tallies quite closely with our day-to-day use of these terms. When, for example, talks about the future of the West Bank between the Palestinians and the Israeli government break down and the parties resort to the use of force (whether of the conventional military kind or the kind used in the *Intifada*), then we customarily talk of the political process having broken down. We then often look forward to a time after the military action when the parties will re-engage in a political process – that is, in discussion about the basic rules of association to be adopted by the parties to the dispute.[27]

It is important to note that this understanding of politics within civil society delinks politics from the *polis* – in particular, it delinks it from the modern form of the *polis*, which is the state. From this viewpoint, engaging in politics is not something which is only (or primarily) done within, or with regard to, the state. People may engage in politics with regard to common rules of association across all the myriad forms of association within which humans live (from families at the micro level to international organizations at the macro level).

This understanding of politics also delinks politics from that kind of 'general will' which is often taken to exist within states. On the view for which I am arguing, politics can take place between those who do not participate in a shared common will at all. Thus, for example, civilians in far-flung places with no connection to the general will which constitutes, for example, the Swaziland monarchy, can participate in a political discussion about the merits of the rules of association which hold that polity together. *For civilians, politics is not an activity confined to those directly involved in the social arrangement whose rules are under discussion.* Civil society opens a place within which all civilians, no matter where they are, may engage in political discussion about, for example, some or all of the following:

- What rules of association would be fair with regard to the Palestinians on the West Bank of the Jordan in Israel. This discussion would involve talk about the possibility of an autonomous status for the Palestinian people within Israel. Here consideration might be given to some form of confederal or federal arrangement. It might also involve discussion of the formation of an independent Palestinian state.
- Discussion about the rules governing the operation of international hedge funds.
- Discussion about the regulation of child labour internationally.
- Discussion about the rules in terms of which men and women worldwide regulate the use and exploitation of the international environment.
- The authority of parents to practice clitordectomy on their female children,
- The practice of witch burning among the Venda in the North Transvaal in South Africa.

(This list could be greatly extended. A complete list would include all forms of human association.)

I wish to terminate the list here in order to highlight one of the most important human associations whose rules may be brought into the political arena for discussion. Civil society creates a space within which the rules of association of the system of states as a whole may be politicized. This is one of the two most powerful social arrangements extant in the modern world (the other being civil society itself). It has a clear set of basic rules as embodied in international law. Civilians may wish to politicize these – to bring them into the political domain for consideration. Many civilians, especially within the camp of post-structural theorists, are currently engaged in doing just this. Questions which may be asked of the existing rules are: Is the arrangement of the world into a system of sovereign states a just arrangement? If it is, is the current number of states the optimum one? Is the present set of states with the existing boundary arrangements appropriate? Should we seek to confederate some or all of the states? What is to be said for proposing federal arrangements for some (or all) of them? Should we abandon the state form altogether in favour of some other governmental structure and, if so, what should this be? Here in civil society, then, is a space for politics which is not contained within the state, and which may indeed challenge the state and the system of states as a whole.

In all this it is imperative to remember that civil society is not made up of like minded individuals who use the space created between them to discuss what to do next. It is not akin to a society of Islamic (Christian, Jewish, Hindu, etc.) people who discuss among themselves what projects they ought to engage in during the next decade. Rights holders in civil society are, concurrently with their participation in civil society, also members of a wide spectrum of nations, religious orders, ethnic groups, cultural movements, and so on. Within these diverse arrangements people hold vastly disparate views about what constitutes a good life. Their participation in civil society gives them a common vantage point from which to politicize (in part or *in toto*) the other associations which they encounter in the world.

There is a sense in which it is misleading to speak of civil society as creating a space within which politics may take place because it does not create a single space, but is better understood as creating a facility within which an unlimited number of political spaces may emerge. Wherever two or more civilians gather together they may engage in politics. By respecting one another's basic rights they create a space in which politics can take place. What rules of which associations are deemed by them to be worthy of politicization will vary hugely from group to group. Some people might be preoccupied with challenging the traditional gender roles in nuclear families. Their discussion might be limited to discussing the family within a narrow area (Britain) or a much wider domain (the West). Others might be interested in the designing of a global regime for the regulation of forest resources. This might involve politicizing the legal systems of specific states, the practices of certain companies, as well as aspects of international law. Yet others, with a narrower focus might confine themselves to disputes about rules regarding the ordination of women within the global domain of the Roman Catholic Church.

In the light of the above it is clear that civil society does not create some centralized public place for politics. It does not create a forum within which all political issues are brought before the attention of all people. It does not create a parliament. What it does is allow for a spontaneous division of labour and of political space according to individual civilians' particular preoccupations. It allows for political discussion to emerge where and when civilians feel it to be needed.

Before the advent of modern technologies of communication most people confined their political activity to the local realm. For it was here that the issues which were pressing for them arose. Nowadays circumstances are substantially different. Modern means of communication have made possible co-operative efforts which span vast distances. These, in turn, depend on forms of association the rules of which can quite readily be expected to become contentious and enter the political realm. As I write, the most spectacular example of this is the discussion which has arisen surrounding what rules should be put in place to regulate the operation of the so called 'hedge funds'.[28] This is not an issue which is only of interest to that small elite who are directly involved in such funds, but is a matter which is of direct interest to millions of civilians worldwide who have money invested in pension schemes, unit trusts, insurance companies, and so on. What happens to the hedge funds has dramatic consequences for many of these. It would not be surprising, then, to find that many such civilians will wish to participate in the political discussion about rules to govern such funds.

The public spaces within civil society are open to all people (both practising civilians and those who are treated by them *as if* they were rights holders).

Anyone wishing to make use of the public space created by civil society for politics may do so. Civilians may not deny someone this right because they are not women, not black, not gay, and so on.

Rights as pre-political

Civil society creates the possibility for a certain kind of politics. It is a kind of politics based on discussion, conversation, dialogue, negotiation, diplomacy, and so on. These activities all require that those participating in them recognize one another as having a basic set of rights such as the rights to safety of the person, free speech, free movement and association. What politics, understood this way, rules out almost completely is the legitimacy of the use of power or force to eradicate, silence or exclude certain voices from the debate. *Civil society is the ground for this kind of politics; it is not itself the result of this form of politics.*[29]

This approach may be contrasted with that presented by Attracta Ingram who argues for a political theory of rights.[30] For her, rights are the outcome or product of a political process in which the citizens in a polity decide on who is to be entitled to what. Her account of human rights presupposes the prior existence of authoritative institutions (most importantly, states) within which the politics that determine what rights people are to have takes place. What I am suggesting is that the language of individual, first generation rights we use points to the existence of a practice within which a politics is possible that is prior to that which takes place in sophisticated social institutions such as states. In the prior practice of civil society, these institutions themselves (the state and the community of states as a whole) are subject to critical scrutiny. Civil society must be understood as a minimalist social institution which, by establishing people as rights holders, makes possible a certain kind of politics between them – makes possible a way in which they can approach disputes about the basic rules of the associations under which they live without resorting to naked power or force.[31]

The subject matters of politics

The rules of association which may be politicized in civil society are the rules of any and all human social formations, from family structures to the institutions of states and international organizations. Some of these are, in terms of our earlier classification, purposive practices. The rules of these might be politicized, for example, when workers insist on profit-sharing arrangements in their pay packages. But, of course, some of the associations under political consideration may be authoritative practices. The basic rules of association of some authoritative practice (such as a religious one, for example) might become a political issue between some civilians who are participants in the religious practice in question and others who are not. An example would be a dispute between Roman Catholics and non Roman Catholics about the sinfulness or not of certain methods of birth control.[32] What the norms of civil society make possible here is the articulation by both parties to this dispute of their respective positions. The Roman Catholics are given, in civil society, an opportunity to explain how for them Roman Catholicism is not a purposive association, but is an authoritative practice within which they are constituted as having certain valued identities. They are accorded a chance to explain the complexities of this practice and how the different parts are related to one another. In like manner, those opposing this position are able to explain to the Roman Catholics how participation in the Catholic practice precludes people from participating in other forms of authoritative practices, such as a secular liberal one. In the ensuing discussion it may come to pass that both parties find their original positions shifting in the light of the discussion which has taken place. Of course, this happy result might not happen. When it does not, the parties will have to discuss possible arrangements which might accommodate their respective points of view.

Civil society, then, makes it possible for members of one authoritative practice to interpret their rules of association to members of other practices, and provides a forum within which the parties may dispute the merits of these. What it does *not* do is provide final criteria (in Rorty's terms, it does not provide a 'final vocabulary') for deciding which of the practices is, in some ultimate sense, better than the others. In other words, I am not putting forward a liberal interpretation of civil society in terms of which all other social arrangements are to be judged merely in terms of the extent to which they protect (or fail to protect) individual human rights, and according to which all other forms of association are to be judged merely in instrumental terms – in terms of how well they promote human rights. On the interpretation of civil society which I have been offering, civilians would not opt for, or endorse, forms of association which undermine the basic rights individuals have in civil society, but they would fully acknowledge the possibility of other forms of human association that civilians might construct which, while not undermining basic rights, nevertheless, might create new forms of human value not found in civil society. Thus some civilians might construct a socialist authoritative practice, others a libertarian authoritative practice, some a nationalist practice, and yet others a social democratic form, and so on.

A possibility worth mentioning is that rights holders in civil society might put together a purposive association (such as the European Iron and Steel Community) which in the fullness of time might become an authoritative practice. It may be that this is how authoritative practices come into being: by starting out as purposive associations which, over time, come to have constitutive ethical significance for those involved in them. We may well, in the not too distant future, see something like this happening with regard to purposive associations formed to deal with environmental problems, with the control of international finance, with the control of international crime syndicates, and the whole question of global poverty. (There may be many other good purposes which will lead to the formation of associations to pursue them.) These may be the precursors of new ethically foundational authoritative practices.[33]

The delegitimation of tradition

I have stressed throughout that civil society as a global practice within which people make claims of first generation human rights against one another is not to be understood as a state of nature which existed before all other forms of association; instead it must be seen as an authoritative practice that has come into being comparatively recently. It is currently growing from strength to strength. In the previous sections, I have been discussing how this practice creates a space wherein the rules of all the associations within which we live (including civil society itself) can be politiciszed – that is, brought up for public discussion.

One of the consequences of the rise of civil society is that it has provided a space from which it is possible to question the legitimacy of many existing practical associations that have long been considered legitimate and even foundational (or, to put the matter conversely, it has raised the possibility of delegitimizing many existing practices). Civil society is potentially corrosive of all existing ethical practices – from patriarchal family systems, feudal land-owning systems, tribal authority structures, the system of sovereign states, traditional church orders, vanguard party structures, systems based on racial privilege and indeed, of course, it even places its own standing as itself open to question. In other words, where people declare themselves to be rights holders in civil society, they put all human formations on notice that they may be subject to political scrutiny. 'Political scrutiny' meaning, in this case, being subject to a public debate in which everybody has a right to participate.

Exclusive practices in an open society

A feature of civil society is that rights holders in it may use their rights to form exclusive practices, subject to the constraints of civil society, yet it remains the case that civil society itself may not be made into an exclusive practice.

Exclusive international practices which rights holders might form may include global associations for rich polo players, international associations for university women, and service organizations such as *Médecins sans Frontières*. The most significant of the exclusive associations which they might form are states and exclusive associations of states such as the Organization of African Unity (OAU), Organization of American States (OAS), Association of Southeast Asian Nations (ASEAN), and so on.

The founders of such associations may establish basic constitutions for these which specify their form and function and include mechanisms and criteria governing the admission of new members. What rights holders, as rights holders, may not do though is set up associations which preclude rights holders exercising their basic rights. This applies to both the rights of those within the association and those external to it. Thus rights holders might set up an association with a carefully defined class of members (it might be a women's association, a religious order, a nationalist movement or a democratic state), but as civilians they may not adopt a constitution which seeks to deprive anyone of their basic rights to speech, assembly, movement, safety of the person, conscience, property, and so on. Thus any civilian who becomes a member of an exclusive association always retains his or her civilian rights to criticize the association, to leave it, to demand that it should not harm his or her person, and so on. In similar fashion, the association may not, in its constitution or in its policies, attempt to deprive those beyond the confines of the association of their first generation rights. What this means is that civilians are committed to rejecting any attempt by any association to deprive individuals of those aspects of their autonomy constituted in civil society. Thus, although individuals are free to join exclusive associations (for polo players, for gays, for women, for hedge fund managers), they are also always free to leave them, criticize their policies and their basic constitutions, hold discussions with other members of the association about the merits of its existence and its activities. Not only are rights holders within the association always entitled to do these things, so too are rights holders who are not members of the exclusive group. They, also, may seek to discuss amongst themselves, or with members, the merits of every aspect of the association. *In short, civil society places limits on what non-intervention rules exclusive associations of civilians may adopt.* For participants in civil society, discussion as a form of intervention is always permissible. Our society of civilians is one which constitutes us, as people who have a right, to be critics of all social forms.

Civil society itself, though, may not transform itself into an exclusive association. This stems from the rule that both active participants in civil society and non-participants are to be treated as rights holders. No person is to be excluded from rights holding. This is a fundamental feature (a constitutive feature) of civil society and is not a policy matter which may be changed from time to time as circumstances change.

Civil society as a site of opposition in international relations

In the light of the above it is clear that global civil society provides a permanent site for legitimate opposition to all forms of associational life. Rights holders may make use of their rights to both question and oppose social formations and the policies pursued by the authorities within them. People in Brazil may voice their concerns at the massacre in Tiananmen Square. Rights holders everywhere were entitled to criticize the form and policies of the apartheid government in South Africa. From the point of view of civil society, anyone (including the governments of China and South Africa) who sought to censor the criticism would have been guilty of unethical conduct. Rights holders are entitled to move beyond criticism to form social movements expressly designed to oppose such events. They are entitled to make use of their right to freedom of the press to publicize their criticisms far and wide.

What criteria (beyond those requiring respect for individual human rights) are to be used in subjecting associations to political criticism is, of course, something about which rights holders might not all agree. The question concerning appropriate criteria of evaluation is likely to be highly contested. Civil society provides a space within which this contest may be held without recourse to violence or force. Use of such methods would infringe individuals' rights. Thus, in the ongoing discussion about the appropriate institutions to be constructed for Kosovo, a political debate will reveal a wide range of opinion about the criteria to be used in setting these up. Some may call for a liberal state which includes the whole of the existing Yugoslavia, others for some modified form of apartheid state in which different peoples are given considerable autonomy, and finally there are sure to be those who call for complete independence for Kosovo. If the participants in this debate within civil society cannot agree on a solution, they may then have a subsequent discussion about the construction of a set of secondary institutions within which the primary constitutional disputes may be dealt with. They may consider making use of the United Nations, or of NATO, or they may decide on the setting up of a contact group of powerful states.

The open society and the limits of force

Civil society, by definition, has no central government. A consequence of this, taken together with the rule that all non-participants are to be treated as if they were rights holders, is that members of civil society seek in their interactions with non-participants to proceed through discussion (the application of the free speech injunction) rather than through the use of force. For rights holders, the only justified use of force occurs in response to those who infringe rights holders' basic rights.

Diversity

A rights-holder society like civil society is one which advances the value of diversity. To acknowledge other people's basic rights is to acknowledge that they have a domain of free choice which they may use as they wish. Rights holders who are Buddhists will make different choices to those who are Christians; those who are hedonists will act differently to ascetics; those who are Serb nationalists will act differently to those who are Kosovan nationalists (and so on through the vast range of final values which humans may choose).

Of particular importance in this regard is the relationship which must hold between we who are rights holders in civil society and those particular exclusive foundational authoritative practices which we know as nations. The interpretation of civil society that I am offering here rejects any stark choice between cosmopolitanism (which valorizes the sovereign individual seen in isolation from any constitutive community), on the one hand, and communitarianism (which stresses that individuals only constitute themselves as beings with moral worth in closed national or religious communities), on the other.[34] Instead, the analysis of civil society which I am offering suggests that we ought to understand civilians to be constituted as who they value themselves to be in a range of social practices over and above civil society. These might include religious and national ones. One can thus be both a civilian and a nationalist.[35]

Wide agenda: strict constraints

As rights holders in civil society we accord one another the opportunity to place the whole of our human associational life on the political agenda. None of the following are sacrosanct from the point of view of civilians:

- Existing forms of states
- Existing boundaries
- The current number of states
- Present international organizations
- Our present way of organizing the international economy
- The list of human rights
- The values presently embedded in international law
- Our current ways of organizing democracies
- The right of any particular nation to self-determination
- Existing nationalist claims
- Existing ethical communities

From the point of view of rights holders, all of the above may be brought into the public domain for political evaluation. Civil society constitutes a global public domain. The constraints on the agenda are minimal. However, there are very severe constraints on how rights holders might proceed with regard to the issues raised. They are not permitted to follow courses of action that would deny to the participants in the political debate their basic individual rights which form the framework for politics.

The limits of civil politics

As we have seen, civil society provides a basic social arrangement from within which people can engage in a political consideration of all other social forms from the smallest to the global. There is, however, a limit to civil politics which is set by the constitutive rules of civil society itself. The limit becomes apparent when we consider the extent to which civil society itself might become the subject matter of civil politics. Let us approach this topic by considering the ways in which civilians might politicize civil society itself.

First, many civilians, from Marx to Nozick, have noted the consequences of the long-term operation of a rights holding practice such as civil society. They have pointed to the unequal pattern of holdings which emerge over time as rights holders interact with one another in the legitimate exercise of their rights.[36] Some civilians might object to the inequalities which emerge over time through the operation of the market and might set about discussing the justice of these outcomes. The most famous discussion along these lines in the last century was that produced by John Rawls in his *Theory of Justice*.[37] In the previous century, Karl Marx provided a different view of the same problem. Another great debate, which still continues, about the pattern of wealth distribution between the North and the South is a variant of this kind of discussion. Any of these interpretations of the effects of the operation of civil society might lead civilians to question the basic rules of civil society itself.

Second, we civilians may wish to discuss the relationships which hold between the authoritative practice within which we are constituted as civilians and other authoritative practices within which we are constituted, such as families, churches, states and the interstate order. This book itself is a contribution to this kind of debate. Another recent example of a contribution by a civilian to this debate is to be found in Robert Bruce Ware's *Hegel*.[38]

There can be no doubt but that civil society makes possible such debates about civil society itself. However, we need to note that civil society allows debates on such questions to follow two paths, both of which have strict limits.

One path which it allows is that of abstract speculation. As civilians we might speculate in a purely abstract way about brave new worlds – about the abolition of civil society itself and the formation of new social orders in which new kinds of actors would be constituted – actors who would be quite different to us (the civilians engaged in such speculation). Here we reach the limit. The formal constraint operative here is that civilians, *qua* civilians, cannot put such speculative ideas into practice. For, by definition, doing this would involve the destruction of civil society within which they (we) are constituted as civilians. People who understand themselves to be beings who hold first generation rights could not as such engage in this kind of project, for in so doing they would be destroying the social practice within which they are constituted as the kind of actor they value themselves to be. Following this path would be either a form of ethical suicide, or a leap of faith into an unknown social constitution.

The other path which civilians might follow is to engage in a political discussion about the rules of association of their own constitutive practice from the point of view of some already established higher order foundational practice within which civil society itself has been subsumed. We may conceive of such a higher order practice as having created new forms of actor which improve on and complement the standing of civilian. This kind of discussion would be about the ethical superstructures built on the base of civil society. This monograph itself is a contribution to this latter kind of discussion, and the next chapter takes the discussion forward in this way.

Concluding remark

In this chapter I have explored some of the major features of global civil society, the society within which we claim ourselves to be the bearers of first generation rights. I have explored these because civil society is a particularly important practice for those of us who make such rights claims for ourselves. It is a foundational authoritative practice. We value ourselves as we do because of our participation in it. This has not been a sociological investigation based on empirical research directed towards describing and explaining civil society. Instead, I have outlined the features of civil society which I believe flow from the rights claims we make for ourselves.

In the next chapter I shall investigate some of the shortcomings of civil society as seen from a higher order rights-based practice which is the society of democratic and democratizing states.

6 Rights in the system of democratic and democratizing states

Constitutive theory sets out to show how we are constituted as ethical beings in a hierarchy of practices where each superior practice may be seen to have solved the shortcomings of the subordinate ones.[1] Constitutive theory does not claim that the subsequent practices are the result of conscious ethical problem-solving activity in the prior practices. It also does not claim that the subordinate practices had built into them a teleological logic which inevitably leads to the emergence of the superior practices. The claim made by constitutive theory is merely that with hindsight we can discern what contribution to our current ethical standing is made by the different practices within which we participate and how certain problems in the subordinate practices were solved in the superior ones. Constitutive theory is a practical example of philosophy painting its grey upon grey after the dusk has fallen and the owl of Minerva has flown.

In this book I am concerned to discuss the role rights play in two of the key practices in the hierarchy within which I and others are constituted as free people, and to examine the tensions between them. In Chapter 5 I discussed several of the remarkable features of global civil society, which is the first of these practices. In it we constitute one another as the holders of first generation individual rights. In that chapter I presented the major features of global civil society in a positive light. I shall turn shortly to a discussion of the ethical shortcomings of this practice as a lead into a more detailed discussion of the second practice – the society of democratic and democratizing states. This, too, is a practice within which rights play a central role, although the rights involved are a different set of rights to the basic rights constituted in civil society. Although the society of democratic and democratizing states must be understood as a single practice, I shall, for the purposes of exposition, first discuss the democratic state as a single entity and then discuss the system of democratic and democratizing states as a whole.

The democratic state as an ethical practice

As citizens in a democratic state we gain an ethical standing which builds upon and improves upon that which we achieve within civil society. A good way of highlighting what we gain within this practice is to consider what we would lack were we confined to civil society and were we denied the standings which we enjoy in democratic states. In order to make apparent what civil society lacks, let us go through an hypothetical exercise in which we imagine ourselves as not having the ethical standings we enjoy as members of democratic states. In what follows two things must be kept in mind. First, it must be remembered that we do not, and never did, live in a pure civil society as I am about to portray it below. People are (and always have been) constituted as ethical beings through their simultaneous participation in a range of, what for them, are ethically foundational practices. Second, in this exercise I portray civil society as having a clear boundary. I do this purely for purposes of exposition. In practice, a defining feature of civil society is that it has no geographical boundaries. This stems from the norm that in civil society civilians are committed to treating all people as civilians whether or not they understand themselves to be such. They do not distinguish between insiders and outsiders.

Ethical shortcomings of civil society

From the point of view of citizens in a democratic state we can discern the ethical problems which would beset us were we merely participants in civil society – were we merely civilians and not citizens.

Alienation

In a pure civil society unencumbered by other ethically foundational practices we would recognize one another as rights holders. Although rights holding would be empowering in many ways, it could also be construed as isolating individuals one from another. A society of rights holders would be a society of individuals bent on protecting their individual spheres of action walled off for them by their basic rights. From the point of view of an individual rights holder, all other rights holders would be potential threats who could at any time attempt to infringe his or her rights. Accordingly, rights holders would need to be ever vigilant for those who would trespass against them. Because rights are held individually, it is the individual him or herself who would always have to be on guard against wrongdoers. There is a sense, then, in which a society of rights holders would be a society of cautious, wary, suspicious people. It would be an alienating social practice.

Competition

To possess rights is to have options. Rights holders have to decide what to do with their rights. They have to decide what to do within that domain of action protected by the rights protecting their person, rights granting them freedom of speech, movement, assembly, contract, conscience, academic inquiry and their right to own property – all of which are established for them within civil society. In a civil society, as I have presented it here, people would exercise their rights in order to link up with other rights holders in arrangements for their mutual advantage. From the point of view of a single rights holder, the field of opportunities would be forever changing as other rights holders forged links for mutual benefit amongst themselves. For such an individual it would always be possible that the use to which other people put their rights would leave him or her worse off. There would be, then, in civil society, a necessary and ongoing element of competition between rights holders as each sought to use his or her rights to best advantage and as each lived in fear of what those in the business world graphically refer to as 'the downside risk.' Here again this suggests that a pure civil society would be an alienating practice.

Individuals in association: expendable means to desired outcomes

Rights holders might use their rights to contract with one another to form associations amongst themselves for mutual advantage. Through contractual arrangements, rights holders might agree, for example, to make things for others, to have sex with them, to teach them, to generate publications for universities, to provide sporting spectacles for others, to merge their assets in order to achieve economies of scale for some group project, to defend one another, and so on. But just as rights holders might make such contracts, they could also rescind them in order to set up different and better contracts with others. The 'we' formed by such contractual arrangements (as in 'We here at General Motors have decided that …') is always, as it were, tentative and provisional. A partner today may be an asset, but tomorrow for some reason (through the invention of some new technology, for example) this could change. The partner might become a liability; the asset could become a burden, and, as such, become discardable. In some measure, then, all parties to such arrangements would be permanently at risk. Here, once again, it is apparent that life in civil society could be alienating. Participants to contracts would always fear the moment at which they might find themselves discarded from some association. Living under such fear would be an alienating condition.

Absence of community

Civil society itself, and the purposive associations which rights holders create in it, are not communities (although some associations might subsequently become such). Rights holders in civil society do not experience civil society itself as a community. Civil society and the associations which rights holders put together in civil society are contractual arrangements created in order to achieve specified purposes. As already mentioned, if the arrangements failed to achieve these they could be dissolved. The rights holders involved are, for one another, merely the means to be used in pursuit of chosen ends. If our lives were confined to this kind of association we would not experience the ethical standing which comes to us through our participation in communities.

Let us consider briefly what might be involved in having such standing – the standing of being a member of a community. In order to do this we need some answers to the question: What is a community? I have in mind here social forms which have all or some of the following features. Within a community members are accorded value simply because they are members, not for what they can contribute to some externally defined purpose. In communities members are often considered to be worthy of support through thick and thin. It is in communities that we experience feelings of solidarity. In the context of communities people come to perform acts of heroism and altruism which are sometimes referred to by philosophers as acts of supererogation. In performing these, people are prepared to suffer hardship and make great sacrifices (including the so-called 'ultimate sacrifice') for the sake of protecting the community's values. In doing these things actors often display great idealism. There are, needless to say, many different kinds of communities. These range from micro communities, like families, through larger ones, such as groups of friends, lodges of Freemasons, churches, tribes, clans and ethnic groups, and on, to very large communities such as nations and nation states.

A pure civil society would not be a social form within which rights holders would experience community and for which rights holders would perform the high-minded deeds of the kind that get done in the name of community. In the purposive associations of civil society, rights holders would not enjoy that standing in terms of which other members would consider themselves honour bound to make sacrifices, do heroic deeds, and so on, for such rights holders. In the associations established within civil society, all that rights holders may expect is that others fulfil their contractual obligations – this expectation is thin indeed when compared with the loyalty, honour-bound dutifulness, heroism, and altruism, which members expect from one another in communities. Insofar as civil society fosters social formations that are not communities but purposive associations, and insofar as it fosters links with others mediated by contract only, it could well be understood as an alienating society.

The limits of self-government in civil society

In a pure civil society, rights holders would have a domain within which they were free to use their rights as they thought fit. There is a sense in which each individual would be self-governing within a circumscribed domain. But from the point of view of an individual rights holder, the overall pattern of exchanges between rights holders would be a contingent one. It would simply be the total set of choices taken by all other rights holders. The resulting pattern of decisions would not be the outcome of a conscious act of self-government by participants acting as members of some social whole. The final pattern of interaction would be an arbitrary one; it would not be an outcome that participants in civil society would regard as having been the result of their communal decision. All this is simply another way of saying that civil society would be, as I mentioned earlier, a society without government. It (civil society) is by definition not a social whole which could be self-governing. Rights holders subject to the arbitrary pattern of contracts as it emerged from multiple transactions would be less than free. They would be less free than they would be under a system where the pattern of relations was determined by them acting in concert with others through some system of self-government.

Rights holders: victims of arbitrary power configurations

This shortcoming of civil society is very similar to that mentioned in the previous section. Rights holders in civil society would find themselves participating in a society in which the contracts made by others could (and probably would) result in patterns of power which would be very unequal. Any single rights holder (or group of rights holders) might find him or herself powerless vis-à-vis some dominant power configuration in the region. For example, an arms manufacturer in South America might find itself at the mercy of huge conglomerates in Europe. Insofar as the basic rights of such a disadvantaged person had not been infringed during the process of power accumulation by other rights holders, they would have no ethical standing vis-à-vis those who were more powerful from which position they might seek redress from the consequences of such inequalities. From the point of view of civil society, no wrong would have been done such an arms dealer. Furthermore, since civil society has no central authority (by definition) and since it has no borders (by definition) there would be no collective entity (and no government of such an entity) to whom the dealer could address a claim that the overall distribution of power was ethically wrong or unjust. No single rights holder and no single group of rights holders would regard themselves as responsible for the overall distributions of power which resulted from rights holders making legitimate use of their rights. With hindsight we can see this to be an ethical flaw in civil society. In it participants would have no means, other than their individual rights, whereby they, as members of the whole, would be able to address gross inequalities generated by the structures within it.

Basic rules: given not chosen

The rules of civil society in terms of which rights holders recognize one another as such, are, from the point of view of any single participant, simply given. They are not the product of any decision procedure in which he or she together with all the other participants either did or could have had a part. There is no way in which individual participants could plausibly claim that the rules constituting civil society were self-imposed or created by them. Thus, although the rights individuals enjoy in civil society constitute them as free people, the rights holders might still see themselves as less than free in that the rights-creating rules might be seen in some broad sense to have been imposed upon them. The contrast here is with the situation which pertains within a democratic state. Here, the citizens understand themselves to be the ultimate source of the authority of the laws embodied in the constitution and the laws which flow from the legislative process created by the constitution.[2]

Another dimension of this matter is that in civil society the rules of the society are not open to amendment by the participants in the rights practice. The list of rights regarded as basic may change in an incremental and informal way over time, but civil society has no government and has no pre-established way for amending the rules which govern the society. In this sense the freedoms established in civil society do not provide the participants in it with the means to amend the rules of their own society. They may discuss amending them, but they lack a central rule making authority which could enact the amendments being discussed. All of this is in sharp contrast to what pertains within a polity such as a democratic state. Here the participants themselves know that they jointly, through certain prescribed procedures, may amend the basic rules of association under which they live.

Civil society: absence of reflectivity amongst rights holders

In civil society although the people know themselves to be rights holders, the rules of the society do not impress upon the participants that as rights holders they are participants in a social practice. For the most part, rights holders are not aware of the part which they play in the constitution of civil society nor are they aware of the role others play in constituting them as rights holders. Being unaware of these matters, rights holders in civil society normally do not contemplate changing the basic rules of their association, for they are not aware that they are participating in an association at all! We might anticipate that in the normal course of events the rules of civil society will be taken to be, in some broad sense, 'natural' – as that which is given.

The limits of ethical criticism from within civil society

There are strict limits to what ethical criticisms would be possible from within civil society itself. These limits to criticism, in turn, limit the range of transformative actions open to rights holders within civil society. The ethical shortcomings of civil society that I have discussed above (and the limitation being discussed in this section itself) are not criticisms which could be generated from within civil society itself were it established in its pure form. The only ethical problems which could arise from within civil society itself (were it the case that this was the only ethically foundational practice in existence) would be those to do with protecting and enforcing basic rights. When rights holders in such a society came to ponder what associations it would be ethically appropriate for them to form, the only constraint on them would be that provided by the authoritative practice from within which they were acting – the constraints imposed on them by civil society itself, the constraint, that is, that they not create associations which infringe basic individual rights.

Within civil society whatever associations rights holders formed would be purposive associations. This is definitionally true. Rights holders would exercise their rights to create associations in order to achieve their purposes. They might establish partnerships, corporations, clubs, associations, states or international organizations. Even were they to create institutional structures which were democratic in form these would be purposive associations.[3] In setting up these many different kinds of association, though, it would remain the case that the only ethical problems for rights holders in civil society would be: how are we to avoid abusing individual rights, and, what institutional forms might we create to protect these basic rights? The whole line of argument developed in Robert Nozick's *Anarchy, State and Utopia* proceeds in this vein. It portrays the process of reasoning which might lead rights holders in a society of rights holders to form a state.[4]

What cannot take place from within civil society itself is the identification of the ethical shortcomings outlined in this chapter or the identification of what social arrangements might be put in place to provide solutions to these. These shortcomings can only be identified with hindsight – from the point of view of some other subsequent authoritative practice which builds on the ethical standings created in the former one. In this chapter I have been identifying the shortcomings of civil society from the point of view of the practice of democratic (and democratizing) states. In the light of the ethical identities we have established for ourselves as citizens within democratic states we can look back and discern what, from an ethical point of view, was missing in civil society. From this vantage point we are able to identify certain aspects of civil society as flaws or shortcomings, but they were not (and could not have been) seen as such by people who were constituted solely in civil society.

It follows, then, that we cannot give an account which shows how the new practice of democratic states arose out of a deliberate process of ethical problem-solving by the rights holders in civil society. The criteria for identifying the ethical shortcomings of civil society are not themselves present in civil society. For rights holders within civil society, the only important ethical question would be about how to protect basic rights. This question would be a guide to all individual conduct, including conduct directed at establishing new associational forms. Insofar as rights holders are social engineers, they would seek to establish purposive associations subject to the constraints already mentioned. In the light of this, it is clear that I am not attempting to provide an account of how states were created by rights holders seeking to rectify the shortcomings of their rights-holding practice. This book is not an historical account of how one ethical practice evolved through the deliberate efforts of those in the practices preceding it. Neither is it a history of ethical development such as that provided by Andrew Linklater.[5] Instead, it is an exploration of the internal architecture of two global practices which are ethically foundational for those who participate in them, together with an exploration of the relationships which hold between the two. It is important to explore this architecture because many, if not most, people are participants in these two practices and few have spelled out the relationships which hold between them.

The ethical contribution of the democratic state

In the light of the ethical shortcomings of civil society mentioned above let me now consider the solutions to these which have been achieved in the system of democratic states.[6] In what follows I am not recounting a story of how one institution replaced and improved upon another – that is, I am not giving an account of how civil society was replaced by the democratic state. Instead, it is an account of how, from our present point of view, with hindsight we can see how one social institution came to supplement and improve upon the ethical standings created in subordinate institutions. Throughout what follows it must be remembered that citizens in democratic states whom I am about to discuss are already civilians; that is, they are well-constituted participants in civil society. The ethical advances achieved through their becoming citizens in democratic states are only available to people who are already rights holders in civil society – to people who are already constituted as civilians.

The centrality of citizenship rights in democratic states

An understanding of citizenship *rights* is central to any understanding of the ethical significance of democratic states. The rights of citizenship are not capacities which democratic states may or may not give to participants within them. The very notion of what constitutes a democratic state requires that we understand that such a state is constituted by citizens who are understood to have a specific set of citizens' rights. The link between the concepts of democratic statehood and citizenship rights is an internal one. It is not possible to understand the one without understanding its relationship to the other.

In a democratic state we are constituted as actors with a set of rights which are additional to those which we hold in civil society. These are the rights of the citizen. In terms of these, as citizens, we have certain courses of action open to us which we may choose to use (or not) as we deem fit.[7] These rights are (like all the rights discussed in this book) property rights in that the holder alone decides whether to use them and in what way he or she wishes to deploy them.

Holding a set of citizenship rights is of major ethical significance for us. Many people engaged in long and bitter struggles to have these rights accorded to them. Others are still immersed in such struggles, as in Palestine, for example. Of particular interest is the way in which gaining these rights solves the ethical shortcomings of civil society. Before turning to a discussion of these solutions, let me outline the nature of citizenship rights and the context in which they are held.

The rights of citizens in democracies

Citizenship rights, as they are currently understood, are always held within that *legal* institution which we know as the democratic state. To hold citizenship rights in a democracy is to understand oneself to be a participant in a social whole with

a determinate, legally defined, membership and a specific kind of legally constituted government. *The primary characteristic of a democracy is the legally defined set of
relationships which hold within it, between citizens (the holders of certain kinds of rights), on
the one hand, and their government, on the other.* In a democracy those who are subject
to government are not the slaves of an owner, the serfs of a lord, or the subjects
of a king, but are citizens – they are people who possess certain kinds of legally
defined rights vis-à-vis one another and vis-à-vis the government of the day. *In a
democracy the relationship between government and citizens (and between the citizens themselves)
is determined by positive law.* It is spelled out in an elaborate legal system which
includes both statutory and common law. The basic law (the constitution which
specifies how the government is to be chosen and the terms according to which it
is to govern) and the government itself derive their authority from the citizens of
the state in question.[8] In democracies specific legal procedures are laid down
which spell out just how citizens may exercise their authority over the constitution and the government which holds power in terms of that constitution.

What makes the constitutional state so important are the following three
features. First, the laws embodied in the legal system which comprise the state
are the authoritative rules which regulate, harmonize, co-ordinate (and so on) the
rules encompassed in the myriad other associations, organizations and institutions within which citizens live their lives. In general, we understand the legal
system of the state to be the framework within which the bulk of associational
life takes place. Families, schools, churches, clubs, universities and corporations
are all subordinate to the rules of the legal system which may be said to be a
system of super rules. In other words, it is a system of sovereign rule. Where a
conflict occurs between, for example, the rules passed by the government of a
university (usually the senate and council) and the government of the state in
which the university is situated, it is the latter which is taken to override the
former. The legal system of a state is at the apex of a hierarchy of rule-governed
arrangements which include schools, universities, clubs, commercial enterprises,
and so on.[9]

Second, the legally constituted government of a democratic state is that body
through which citizens decide what rights to grant themselves with regard to the
redistribution of socially generated resources. It is through the mechanisms of
the democratically chosen government that citizens decide on what second
generation rights to accord themselves. These are rights such as the rights to
social welfare, education, health, housing, old age care and basic infrastructure.
These second generation rights are often referred to as 'positive rights' to distinguish them from first generation rights, often called 'negative liberties'. In terms
of the analysis which I am offering here, it is important to note that positive
rights only make sense when they are located in a system of positive law which
specifies a legally constituted government against which such positive rights may
be claimed. Positive rights logically presuppose positive law in a way that negative liberties do not.

Third, it is the constitutional state which determines what rights citizens are
to have with regard to the protection of cultural, ethnic and national forms of

life. Typically, governments in democracies might decide to accord certain special protections towards the languages of cultural minorities within the state.

The distinguishing feature of a *democratic state* is not that it provides a system of law which is authoritative over other systems of rule (this is a defining feature of all sovereign states), but that it provides an overarching set of rules which itself is subject to the ongoing authority of the citizens constituted in terms of those rules. The authority of citizens in a democracy is embodied in a complex set of *individual rights* which typically include the following: the right to equal treatment under the law, the right to stand for election to serve in the different branches of government for fixed terms of office; the right to participate in such elections by voting for the candidate or party of one's choice; the right to form political parties to contest elections; a set of rights enabling the citizens to participate in holding their government to account (through, for example, direct contact with elected office bearers, through the use of an open press, through the use of information freely available from the civil service, etc.); a right to a specified share of whatever welfare benefits (schooling, pensions, housing, health, etc.) which are provided by the elected government to its citizens, and so on. Most importantly, citizens have a right to have their basic rights (which they have as members of civil society) protected and enforced by their government (which is but another way of saying that they have a positive right granted them by the state as citizens to have their negative liberties, their rights as civilians, protected).[10] As particular democracies evolve, the duly elected governments might enact ever more elaborate laws granting further avenues of democratic participation to citizens. In such cases citizens use their citizenship rights to grant themselves further citizenship rights. For example, democratically elected governments might pass laws giving citizens standing for election, a right of access to government funding to finance their election campaigns and it might give citizens the right to the free use of publicly owned media to further their election campaigns.

I have mentioned that a defining feature of democratic states is that within them citizens are accorded a specific set of citizenship rights and that these citizenship rights are *always* to be understood within the context of specific *legal systems*. It is important to expand on the notion of a legal system.

A mature legal system typically has several important features worthy of mention. First, it spells out who falls within its jurisdiction and who does not. Note that not all the people subject to the law of a legal system are citizens: some may be legal migrant workers, others tourists, others foreign nationals with residence permits, such as ex heads of states from foreign countries, and so on. But the point stands – it is not possible to make sense of citizenship rights outside the context of a specific legal system which specifies who falls within its jurisdiction and who does not. Of course, a single person may be a citizen of more than one state, but this does not undermine the central point being made here. As things currently stand the jurisdiction of legal systems is normally defined with reference to a clearly demarcated territory and the people within it. This, though, is not always the case and may be even less so in future. The laws of some legal systems are often binding upon those not living in the territory subject to that law.[11] Although residence within a territory may not always be the primary determinant of who is subject to the law and who is a citizen within a given legal system, it is nevertheless true that a legal system specifies with a high degree of precision who is subject to its jurisdiction.

Second, legal systems are elaborate arrangements of different kinds of law. Besides the *primary laws* which specify how people within the legal system ought to behave (e.g. 'All vehicles on public highways are to be driven on the left-hand side of the road'), within a legal system there are secondary *rules of recognition* which determine how those subject to the law are to identify what the law is. Rules of recognition often include elaborate conventions about what are to count as sources of the common law, such as rules specifying the marks by which citizens can recognize which laws have been properly enacted, and which texts must be taken as authoritative. Often rules of recognition are embedded in constitutional documents.[12]

Third, a legal system typically also has a well-established set of *rules for the adjudication of disputes* which specifies how legal disputes are to be resolved and how people who break the law are to be dealt with. These rules are, in turn, backed by legally defined and controlled instruments for the enforcement of the decisions arrived at through the judicial process.

Fourth, beyond such rules of recognition and adjudication legal systems also have *rules governing the creation of new law*. These govern the process of law creation itself – they spell out how new laws are to be made. These may specify a legislative and/or a judicial process of law creation. In the latter case, it is made clear how new law may be created through the use of precedent. Here precise guides are given as to which courts are entitled to set precedents.

Fifth, and finally, legal systems also specify how constitutional amendments are to be made. Here we have law regulating its own creation at the very highest level. What necessitates these sophisticated arrangements within legal systems is the requirement by participants in complex modern democracies for legal certainty. In order to get on with their complex sets of activities and to co-ordinate them, people need to know with certainty where they stand with regard to the law. There are two aspects to this need for certainty: first, there is the need to have a decision as to how things stand legally with regard to a certain contentious matter. Second, there is the need to know that whatever decision is arrived at it will be effectively enforced in a legally recognized manner.

Importantly, a legal system provides a framework regulating what rules and regulations other associations are entitled to make. In order to achieve the level of certainty necessary for the fluent operation of complex societies, legal systems establish a hierarchy of legal authority such that those who are subject to the law know that the ordinances of cities are subject to the higher-level laws made by provincial legislatures, which in turn are subject to the higher-level laws made by national governments, which in turn are subject to the laws embedded in the constitution of the democratic state.[13] *To repeat, developed legal systems create a high degree of legal certainty in the practice of practices which is the modern democratic state.* This level of legal certainty in turn makes it possible for modern states and the citizens in them to realize a whole range of goals which would not be possible without such legal systems. It also makes it possible for those outside the state to know where they stand legally with regard to their dealings with people within the state in question.

Citizenship rights are held within the context of specific legal systems. Unlike the basic rights of civil society which we consider ourselves to hold whether or not a legal system exists (we consider ourselves to hold them, that is, even in circumstances of anarchy – even where there is no government, judiciary, or legislature), citizenship rights are a component of and are embedded in legal systems in all their sophistication. Let us look more closely at the contrast between the rights of civilians (rights held by citizens in civil society) and the rights of citizens. The basic rights of participants in civil society are rights which may be respected even though the individual participants are not closely involved with one another, do not live near one another, are not subject to the same legal system and are not subject to a common government. Citizenship rights presuppose a much closer set of relationships. Citizens are related to one another in a complex arrangement for self-government under law within a given territory. It is only in such elaborate legal arrangement that the ethical shortcomings of civil society can be overcome and the ethical advances achieved in democracy can come about.

I am claiming then the very notion of democratic statehood entails the notion of citizenship rights, and that such rights must always be understood as being embedded in a legal system consisting of at least primary rules, supplemented by higher-order rules of recognition, adjudication and law creation. If there is this close link between democratic statehood, citizenship rights and legal systems, then this has important implications for those interested in the expansion of democracy beyond state boundaries.[14] Extending the rights of democratic citizenship, then, would require extending the legal system, and this would require subordinating existing legal orders to this new 'stretched' democratic order with state-like features. In particular it would requires the 'certainty creating' features which I have just discussed. The extended legal system ('the extended state', if you like) would not need to subordinate all aspects of the existing democratic states to its sovereignty. It might be crafted so that only certain of its laws were sovereign over those of the existing states. This is precisely what has happened within the European Union. There are specific domains within which EU law trumps domestic legislation. In other words, there is a real sense in which the EU is a supra-state. European citizenship is constituted within this new supra-state legal arrangement.

Democratic states as circumscribed communities: the need for borders

Democratic states consist of citizens who govern themselves through the mechanisms of representative institutions as defined by law. Through these institutions citizens are able to arrange and fine-tune their complicated systems of production, distribution and consumption. They are able to set up elaborate arrangements for collecting taxes and for spending them on the provision of a wide range of social services of one kind or another. These include education, family support, medical care, postal services, defence, old age care, welfare for the weak, sick and unemployed, and so on. Inevitably the range of services which citizens would like to have their governments provide for them outstrips the resources governments have available to them. The balancing act for governments is to determine what level of taxation the voting public will accept in return for what level of services. A crucial requirement throughout this ongoing deliberation between citizens and their government about taxes and services in democratic states *is that the identities and the total number of citizens within the state be known with some certainty. Governments have to make a distinction between insiders and outsiders.* No planned policy that matches taxes to services is possible without precise knowledge of how many are to be taxed and how many are to be served. What is also required is that the state have available to it mechanisms for regulating the number of citizens in a state so as to avoid wild swings in the total which would make planning more or less impossible. For this reason democratic states (and larger democratic entities such as the EU) need some measure of control over their memberships. The standard way in which this is done is through geographical border controls to monitor flows of people in and out of the area of services by registering births and deaths, by conducting regular censuses, by maintaining voters' rolls, and through the operation of formal procedures for accepting new citizens into the body politic.

Citizenship rights: overcoming the ethical shortcomings of civil society

Let me now turn to a discussion of the ways in which we, as the holders of citizenship rights within a democratic state, have overcome the ethical problems of civil society that I enumerated at the beginning of this chapter. The central points can be easily stated:

- Whereas in civil society we were alienated from one another in not clearly understanding ourselves to be part of a social whole, as holders of citizenship rights in a democracy we understand ourselves to be fellow citizens in a clearly defined social entity, the democratic state. Part of understanding ourselves as holders of citizenship rights is understanding that, as such, we are equal, and as equals we are the primary constitutive elements of the democratic state in question. It is clear that this valued ethical status depends on the recognition we give one another within the context of the democratic state. In this knowledge of ourselves as equal co-members of a democratic whole, we are not alienated from one another, but united in consciously conferring on one another this valued ethical standing.
- In civil society we are placed in a relation of possible (and probable) competition with all other rights holders (for example, if I win the hand of the

partner I desire, you don't, if I win the competition for the Chair of International Relations you do not, if my company wins the tender to transport nuclear waste to Australia, yours does not, and so on). In contrast to this, as citizens in a democratic state, we are constituted as equals who have the common interest of advancing the well-being of our state. This is not a zero sum game. That competitive elections are the way in which key decisions are made in democracies does not undermine this point. In democratic elections those competing for office seek to convince all the voters that their policies will secure the interests of all citizens.

• Whereas in civil society we were alienated in that we feared that at any point we might be jettisoned from the purposive associations in which we were involved (for example, this might happen to us because we had not produced our quota of cars in a factory, publications in a university, goals for a professional soccer team, hit records for the record company, etc.) in the democratic state we suffer no such chronic fear of exclusion. In a democracy we are accorded value by our fellow citizens (and we accord value to them) by having our citizenship rights recognized (and by recognizing them in others). This valuing is not accorded to us for what we have done, but simply because we are citizens. In a democratic state (within certain broad parameters relating to treason) our status as citizens is secure. Citizenship (like membership of a family) is not based on a contract which may be summarily terminated by co-contractors because we have failed to perform certain functions. Citizens do not have to produce quotas of x in order to remain citizens; citizens do not compete for tenure.

• In civil society we experience alienation in that we know that if we are excluded from some (or all) purposive associations by our fellow rights holders we shall then be left to our own devices. Beyond respecting our basic rights no one will care for us and we shall be reduced to self-help. This form of alienation is overcome within the democratic state within which, as holders of citizenship rights, we know that our fellow citizens have a responsibility towards us that extends beyond according to us such bare negative liberties.[15] We consider ourselves part of a community of citizens. As citizens of a democratic state we consider ourselves in some broad sense to be responsible for one another's well-being; we understand ourselves to be members of a whole which has an obligation to pay attention to our interests. As citizens we have the ethical standing of people who are entitled to have their interests considered by the other citizens acting in concert through their/our government. What this means is that when a citizen or group of citizens is suffering some hardship they may put a case to the democratic polity as a whole (through the media or directly to the government) requesting that the polity consider their plight, and that an appropriate plan (given the circumstances and the resources available) be made to remedy the problem. In such circumstances we understand ourselves to be addressing our fellow citizens who recognize that they have special obligations towards us; that they are called upon to make some response to our request; that they are in some broad sense responsible for us. In any given case we may not get the response we want, but what our fellow citizens may not do is ignore us or reply that our plight is simply not their concern.[16] In response to our request our fellow citizens might provide some or all of the following: basic protection of civil society rights, positive rights to security, welfare, education, health care, old age care, the use of basic infrastructure, and so on. In deciding what to do in each case governments in democracies have to devise policies which will be in the interests of all the citizens. They are not entitled to simply ignore the interests of a certain section of the citizenry (women, blacks, Jews, Islamic people, etc.).

- In the democratic state citizens gain a sense of themselves as together being engaged in a form of self-government. This moves far beyond the limited self-government of private affairs available to rights holders in civil society. In an election citizens know themselves to be participating in a process to elect the government which is the sovereign law-making body with regard to the vast bulk of issues in their daily lives.[17]

- In civil society from the point of view of an individual rights holder, the overall pattern of outcomes which resulted from rights holders exercising their rights would be experienced as contingent, something which merely happened, and as something beyond their right to control. The individual rights holders would feel themselves to be at the mercy of forces beyond their control (like the weather). A remedy for these ills of civil society is provided in the democratic state within which citizens, through their elected government, in some measure come to control that overall pattern of outcomes. Via legislation the citizens can provide relief for those who have been particularly hard hit by the arbitrary pattern of outcomes realized in civil society. The government can embark on minor or major programmes of redistribution.

- Citizens in democracies do not only know themselves to be the basic participants in a process of self-government, but they understand themselves to be the basic determiners of the constitution in terms of which these law-making procedures themselves are undertaken. Constitutional change itself is in their hands.

- Citizens of democratic states confer upon one another that extraordinarily high ethical standing which is to be someone from whom acts of altruism, self-sacrifice and heroism might be expected (and one whose acts in that vein would be appreciated were they to be carried out). In civil society, a rights holder who carried out such acts in the absence of a specific contract to do so would simply be considered irrational – as acting contrary to his or her self-interest. In contrast, where citizens forfeit their own well-being for that of their fellow citizens, this is considered a reason to accord them honour rather than derision.[18]

- In democracies, citizens are constituted as ethical beings who can be the *recipients* of the ethical acts under the following rubrics (and they themselves can undertake such acts): acts showing fraternal feeling with fellow citizens;

acts of loyalty, altruism, heroism, self-sacrifice towards the democratic state; acts defending the honour of the state; acts which reflect the glory of the whole within which the citizen is but a part (here I have in mind, for example, great performances in international sport, culture, etc.), and so on. In all these cases, the acts of individuals gain their significance in relation to the social whole – the total body of citizens who make up the democratic state. There have in the past, of course, been other social entities within which members would undertake such acts in the name of the whole. These include tribes, clans, churches, nations and states. In all these, though, the actors were not concurrently rights holders in a borderless civil society. What makes the democratic state unique is that it makes possible these ethical standings and these kinds of ethical action amongst people who are at the same time constituted as rights holders within a borderless global civil society.

- As holders of citizenship rights within a democracy people mutually create between themselves an important form of equality which exists concurrently with what are often great inequalities realized between them within civil society. As mentioned earlier in civil society, through civilians making use of their rights over a period of time, a pattern of holdings will emerge which is likely to be hugely unequal. People, equal in their basic civil liberties, will end up unequal in their social positions. On becoming citizens of a democratic state such people are reconstituted as equals in important ways. In the affairs of a democratic state each citizen is accorded equal voting rights, each is accorded an equal right to stand for election to office, each is accorded an equal right to put his or her case to government, each is entitled to equal treatment under the law, and so on. With regard to these matters it is, in principle, of no significance whether one is born into an aristocracy or not, whether one is rich or poor, whether one is educated or uneducated, whether one is male or female, black or white. If the government of a democracy passes a law entitling all mothers to a childcare allowance then all mothers are to be treated equally irrespective of their religion, education, etc. Within the democratic state each citizen is entitled to equal concern and respect as citizen.

- A weakness of civil society in its pure form is that it lacks the institutional machinery to enforce the important ethical value which is created within it – the standing of being a holder of first generation rights. This weakness is remedied by democratic states. In them citizens normally configure their state in such a way that it has as one of its main objectives that of providing the full protection of the law to the rights held by civilians in civil society. Where citizens do this, we have a superior ethical practice reinforcing and consolidating the achievements of a prior ethical practice. This can be expressed as follows: citizens in a democracy may use the machinery of the state (law, legislature, judiciary, executive, police) to strengthen and make actual the rights they have in civil society. They may do this by entrenching these rights in the constitution of their state, by providing for a constitutional court to vet new legislation against the template of such Bills of Rights, and by developing a jurisprudence through legislation and precedent which will ensure that they are not only able to claim their rights, but will be in a position to exercise them in practice. It is important to notice, though, that any given state will only be able to do this with regard to some portion of civil society, for, by definition, no state encompasses the whole of it. Thus, citizens in a democracy in South Africa have been able to use the apparatus of their state to protect the ethical gains of civil society in the territory it occupies, and the citizens of France have used their state to do this in France (and so on). States do not create separate civil societies, but are the guardians of that portion of global civil society which falls within their territorial jurisdiction.[19] Of course, several states may team up to use their enforcement machinery to protect civilian rights internationally. They might do this by creating an International Court of Criminal Justice.

- Those who hold citizenship rights within democratic states regain elements of community and fraternity, certain forms of equality, and certain valued relationships of individuals towards the whole, which were not to be had within the arrangements of civil society. In the democratic state these ethical relationships are realized not by ties of sentiment between particular individuals who know one another well or through sets of distinct interpersonal obligations, but are ties of sentiment to all those who occupy a legally defined role, that of citizen.

- As mentioned earlier, in civil society there is no mechanism whereby participants can, as it were, be collectively reflective about civil society itself. This ethical shortcoming is solved within the democratic state and through the establishment of the constitutionalism required for its existence. Constitutionalism requires of citizens that they be self-conscious about the constitution of the democratic state within which they are participating. This opens the way for them to consider transforming it. As an example of such reflectivity demonstrated in practice consider, for example, the citizens of Great Britain who have recently considered and have agreed to the granting of greater independence to Scotland and Wales. Furthermore, consider how the new government has set itself to incorporate the EU Bill of Rights into the British constitution and to introduce a new electoral system which will secure proportional representation. Democratic states are ideally suited to advance such forms of reflectivity. Most democratic constitutions have built-in measures through which self-reflection (and the resultant transformations) may take place without reverting to pre-constitutional forms of government – forms of government not subject to the self-reflectivity entailed in constitutionalism.

- As a system of government which encourages self-reflectivity, democratic states are also set up to be self-reflective about their own ethical standing. They provide public forums, party platforms, press freedoms, and so on, which are essential for any deep-seated consideration of the ethical bases of the democratic state itself.

Civilian rights and citizenship rights

The picture that I have set out above is one through which rights holders in civil society (civilians) gain added ethical standing by becoming citizens within a democratic state which is itself but a component of the wider practice of democratic and democratizing states. On this view the state is not, as liberals would have it, merely a mechanism whereby the ethical rights created in civil society are protected. Instead, its great ethical significance is that it creates ethical statuses not available to people in civil society on its own. What is being offered in this text, then, is not an account of how the rights citizens enjoy in democratic states are somehow *derived* from the rights which they have in some state of nature. What is being offered is an account of how the freedom enjoyed by people constituted as rights holders in civil society is augmented through their concurrently being constituted as holders of a different set of rights (citizenship rights) in the wider practice of democratic states. One set of rights (civilian rights) is supplemented by another set of rights (the rights of citizens). For this account of *ethical supplementation* to work, it must be shown that the sets of rights established in the two institutions are compatible. It must be shown that it is not the case that the set of citizenship rights created in democratic states undermines or eradicates the rights enjoyed by civilians within civil society. To use Hillel Steiner's phrase, such rights must be compossible.[20]

My whole case rests on the claim that our ordinary language about these two sets of rights supports the account which I am presenting here. Thus, for example, we who claim ourselves to be the possessors of such rights customarily talk of our rights in civil society as being compatible with our rights in the democratic state. For example, as a citizen in the democratic state of South Africa, I describe myself as having a full set of citizenship rights which entitle me to stand for office, to participate in the elections and to hold the elected government to account. But, concurrent with my describing myself as the possessor of these rights of the citizen, I claim for myself all the basic first generation rights accorded to me in civil society: my rights of the person, my rights to free speech, association, contract, movement, conscience, academic freedom, and so on. I and my fellow South African citizens approved a constitution which entrenches these fundamental rights. By so doing we removed these rights from the realm of items which may be placed on the day-to-day legislative agenda. In terms of this constitution, the state may not tamper with these rights and, what is more, it is given the specific task, via the Human Rights Commission, of making sure that the basic rights of South Africans are protected. This is true for South Africa and, in general, is true for all developed democracies. In these, the citizens understand that limits have been placed on what may be brought onto the political agenda – basic rights are put beyond its reach. Governments of democracies are not at liberty to pass legislation curbing citizens' basic rights.

Furthermore, in our ordinary language we who claim ourselves to be the holders of citizens' rights within democratic states do not consider that in making this claim we are denying to those beyond the borders of our state recognition of their basic civil society rights. Quite the contrary, new democracies typically take steps to indicate their formal recognition of the great international instruments for the protection of human rights globally. They do this, *inter alia*, through the signing of the relevant treaties. Were citizenship rights within a particular state incompatible with civilian rights beyond the borders of that state, we would expect to find citizens (and their governments) in new democratic states overtly, regularly and systematically articulating positions in which they made it clear that they no longer recognized the individual rights of those beyond their new state's borders. We citizens do not generally make this kind of claim. This counter-factual supports my case.

The distinction between basic civil society rights and citizenship rights and the compatibility of the two is starkly brought out within the European Union. In the EU citizens enjoy their democratic rights within discrete states, but their civil society rights are respected Europe-wide. As rights holders in civil society, members of the EU may move about at will, speak freely, associate freely, form contracts as they wish and transfer their property at will. No democratically elected government of a member state may pass legislation which threatens the basic rights of anyone in the Union.

Citizenship rights and the society of democratic states

In the foregoing sections I have been discussing how we gain new ethical standing when we acquire citizenship rights within a democratic state. Using myself as an example, I recounted how my becoming a holder of citizenship rights within a democratic South Africa improved upon the ethical standing which I would have enjoyed were I exclusively constituted as a civilian in civil society. In the account given thus far I have been focusing on the people within a single democratic state. This could be read as suggesting that the ethical advances being discussed are such that they are only possible between people within the same democratic state; that while ethical advance takes place within democratic states, the relationships which hold between people who live in different democratic states remains at best at the more rudimentary ethical level of civil society. On this reading, while I might achieve full ethical standing with regard to my fellow South African citizens, I would only be in an ethical relationship with people outside South Africa inasmuch as they and I are participants together in civil society. Interpreting our involvement in these institutions in this way soon leads to the well known communitarian position according to which we have 'thick' ethical relationships with those within our own nation states, whereas, with regards to those beyond the borders of our states, we are at best only in some form of 'thin' ethical bond.[21] This is quite contrary to the interpretation I am putting forward here. Here, I shall make the case that the ethical gain achieved when we become citizens of democratic states is not only a gain enjoyed which we enjoy vis-à-vis those who are our co-citizens within a given state, but is also a gain enjoyed which we as citizens in one state enjoy vis-à-vis citizens in other states. Let me elaborate.

In civil society conceived of in abstraction from other forms of *Sittlichkeit* we would suffer the ethical drawbacks outlined above. These are overcome when we civil society rights holders come to recognize one another as the holders of citizenship rights within democratic states. *This ethical advance does not require that civilians become citizens in the same democratic state.* What is required is that civilians come to recognize one another as people who are citizens within some state in a community of states. The advance is achieved even if we do not live in the same democratic state. For example, it is achieved when you come to recognize me as a citizen in the South African democratic state and I come to recognize you as a citizen in, for example, the French democratic state. The ethical statuses achieved through our mutual recognition of one another as citizens within these democratic states are not eroded by the fact that, in some measure, our states are in competition with one another (for example, through trying to maximize their respective shares of the international arms trade). What matters here is that I recognize you as a being whose status as a free individual is (and can only be) realized within the context of some democratic state; that I recognize that you are not only an isolated individual in civil society who is alienated in the ways mentioned above, but that you are one who finds his or her meaning within the elaborate legal structures of a democratic state within which you are a citizen of equal worth with other citizens, irrespective of your gender, race, religious affiliation, age, family, or wealth; that I recognize you as one who is able, together with your fellow citizens, to govern yourself in terms of constitutionally prescribed forms; that as a citizen you are one who would yourself be prepared to make sacrifices, to be heroic, and to be loyal vis-à-vis your fellow citizens; that you, as a citizen, would understand your fellow citizens doing such things for you; that you understand yourself to be part of a citizenry which might decide through the democratic process to grant to themselves, as citizens within a given democracy, certain second generation rights (rights that require certain forms of redistribution within the polity of those resources that come into being when citizens agree to tax themselves and to use the tax revenues to provide some, or all, fellow citizens with certain services, such as education, healthcare, medical care and so on).[22]

It is important to note what is being excluded here. In setting up an international system within which we recognize one another as citizens in democratic states we are excluding alternative systems such as those which would pertain were we to set up empires within which those in the metropole looked upon those in the colonies as people of less worth; such as those in which an aggressor power subjected those who had been conquered to direct rule without allowing the conquered any participation in government; such as those which existed between great powers and the mandates over which they had been granted authority by some international organization; such as those where peoples and territories are held in trusteeship by great powers acting on behalf of an international body. The society of democratic and democratizing states is not at all like these social forms. In this democratic social formation, although I might not be in the same democratic state as you, we both accord one another a certain kind of ethical standing – that of being individuals worthy of participating as equals in the self-government of the sovereign democratic states within which we live. You in yours, and I in mine.

Where we recognize one another as citizens in democratic states, we are indicating to one another that we are rejecting a whole slew of international modes of conduct which have been used by states against one another down the centuries:

1   We are indicating to one another that we reject wars aimed at territorial expansion into the territories of other democratic states. If you are a citizen in a democratic state which is sovereign within a given territory it is for you and your fellow citizens to decide through the democratic process whether you wish to amalgamate your democratic state with the one in which I live, and vice versa. Were my democratic state to simply invade yours in an aggressive act of expansion this would indicate that I was treating you as one whom it would be appropriate to subjugate. This is the opposite of what is involved in treating you as a citizen in a democracy.

2   We are indicating to one another that we are opposed to systems of international relations based on secret diplomacy between governments. As democrats we are committed to open government – to a form of government where the citizens are able to hold government to account for its deeds. This is only possible where citizens know what their governments are doing – only possible where there is open government. The language of democratic citizenship does not sit easily with the world of secret ententes, and understandings for these might be used by elites to undermine democratic rule. The language we use calls upon us to judge democracies, not only our own, by the extent to which they constitute a system within which open government can take place. We judge the level of democratization in states beyond the borders of our own by, amongst other things, the extent to which their governments are open. For us to make this judgement, they have to be open to scrutiny, not merely to their own citizens, but to us foreigners too.[23]

3   Citizens in democracies seek to bypass ad hoc forms of international relations. Instead, we favour forms which are based on the establishment of firm and predictable international laws. We do this because without such a system of law the recognition which we receive from other democracies would not be secured, but would in some measure be contingent on the whim of those states and the people in them. We would have no assurance that we would continue getting recognition as citizens in free states. Also, systems of law make possible planned and predictable forms of co-operation between citizens in free states.

4   As citizens in free states we are committed to upholding the non-intervention rule, which is a central feature of international law. We do this out of respect for the democratic autonomy of citizens elsewhere in their states. The non-intervention rule is not one which springs up between democratic

states as a practical *modus vivendi*. It is rather a defining feature of the practice of democratic free states. But the non-intervention norm itself is conditional upon democratic states respecting the rights of civilians, which is a precondition for the establishment of democracy and citizenship rights.

Constituting diversity as a value

A major feature of that *Sittlichkeit* which is established when we come to recognize one another as citizens within a range of democratic states is the way in which it accommodates diversity. Where thousands of millions of people recognize one another as citizens within the almost two hundred democratic and democratizing states, part of what is established is a system within which the participants acknowledge that different sets of citizens within different democracies are entitled to use their autonomous powers of self-government in diverse ways. Within one state the citizens through their elected government might decide to set in place a social democracy, within another citizens might arrange things along libertarian lines, within a third they could opt for a socialist arrangement, in a fourth it might be communist, a fifth might opt for a union, a sixth for a federation, and so on. In different democracies citizens might establish for themselves different sets of positive (second generation) rights with which to supplement the negative (first generation) rights they already possess as participants in global civil society.

In the different democratic states citizens might opt for any number of institutional ways with which to accommodate the diverse national, ethnic, cultural and language groups living within the territory of the states in question. Within some the citizens might opt for proportional representation in common legislative bodies, in others they might choose cantonal autonomy, whilst in others they might opt for entrenched forms of over-representation for key minority groups. In becoming citizens in a practice of democratic states, we become participants in a social formation which allows for such diversity to emerge. In this practice we become participants in an ethically authoritative practice within which diversity is constituted as a value.

Thus, we see that diversity is a value which is central to the practice of democratic free states. The whole notion of individuals having citizenship rights which entitle them to participate in setting up states, choosing governments for them and holding their governments to account, is premised upon the knowledge that not all citizens will think alike. Democratic citizenship allows people with widely divergent views to participate in the establishment and government of a wide range of different styles of free state. To value citizenship is to value diversity.

A practice enabling of a more sophisticated global politics

The practice of democratic and democratizing free states may be understood as a social arrangement which makes possible a more sophisticated form of politics than that which is enabled by civil society alone. The definition of politics which I have adopted and which fits well with our normal use of the term is: politics is what we do and say with a view to maintaining or changing the basic rules of the social practices within which we are constituted as actors. In the practice of civil society, by constituting one another as rights holders we effectively depoliticize certain kinds of action and thereby make a politics of diversity possible. We establish amongst ourselves that our basic first generation rights are trumps and are not eligible to be made the subject of politics. By doing this, we bring into existence a framework for politics with regard to all the other social formations within we are constituted. By respecting people's rights, we create a space from which each individual may participate in political activities with a view to maintaining, changing or creating social institutions in ways which seem important to him or her.

Within the practice of free democratic states, we, as citizens, confer upon one another a standing which makes it possible for us to participate in a more sophisticated form of politics not found in civil society in its pure form. As citizens we get to participate in a structured form of decision-making with others about the rules of the associations under which we live. Thus, for example, as a South African citizen by using all the citizenship rights available to me, I get to participate, together with my fellow South African citizens, in decisions about the existing and future legal structure of the South African democracy. Furthermore, we who are citizens in this polity also get to participate in decision-making about the place of our polity, South Africa, in the wider practice of states – in discussions such as that introduced by President Mbeki about an 'African Renaissance'.

Citizenship rights in the wide practice of democratic and democratizing free states entitle us, as participants in democracies, to publicly reflect on the constitutional form of our own state and on the constitutional structure of the practice of states as a whole. From within the framework of our immediate polity, the democratic state, we are entitled as citizens to contemplate and seek for change in the international system as a whole. As co-participants in such a polity, we have an ethically protected place from which we are entitled to engage in domestic and international politics.

Given that people come from widely different social backgrounds and vary greatly in temperament, it is to be expected that citizens making use of their citizenships' rights may from time to time (or, indeed, may often) decide to change the law in various ways. More dramatically, they may use their rights to change the very constitution of their democratic state. Most dramatically of all, they may use their rights to dissolve their existing state and to create one or more new states. Similarly, adjacent democracies might decide to allow a portion of each to secede to form one or more new democratic state(s). Citizens, though, are constrained in the ways they may legitimately go about advocating and pushing for such changes.

As citizens we are constituted as rights holders of a certain kind within a democratic polity. Thus constituted we enjoy an ethical standing not to be had in any other way. However, being constituted in this way places constraints on what we may do. Thus, for example, when some of the citizens of a democracy such as Britain decide that they wish to engage in politics with a view to securing a greater measure of autonomy for Scotland, possibly even full independence, then, as citizens, they are ethically constrained as follows: they are not entitled to simply establish an independent Scotland by force of arms. Doing this would show them to be flouting a fundamental requirement of the British citizenship which they currently enjoy – it would flout the requirement that insofar as they are recognized as the holders of citizenship rights, they are required to recognize the citizenship rights of those who grant them this recognition – their fellow British citizens (and, of course, citizens in other democracies). Citizenship is a relationship of reciprocal recognition. *This constraint, in effect, imposes a procedural norm on those citizens who would change the existing form of the practice of free states (by, for example, creating new states through the break-up or the amalgamation of the existing ones).* It requires of them that they hold to the procedures for constitutional change laid down in the existing global practice within which they currently enjoy citizenship rights. Knowing this, the Scottish National Party has indeed conducted its campaign for the independence of Scotland in a way that scrupulously abides by the methods required by the British constitution, which, in turn, is recognized by the other democracies in the wider practice of states.

Those citizens of Britain who are opposed to independence for Scotland are, as the holders of citizenship rights, similarly constrained in what it would be ethical for them to do in order to prevent a Scottish breakaway. For example: they would not be entitled to prevent fellow citizens bringing this item onto the parliamentary agenda; they would not be entitled to ban parties which seek to promote independence for Scotland; they would not be entitled to imprison leaders who strove for this goal; and so on. As holders of citizenship rights within an existing democracy, they are bound to respect the citizenship rights of the fellow citizens who are advocating secession for Scotland. In short, they, too, are in effect bound to follow a specified set of political procedures. They are required to allow the public promotion of this goal (independence for Scotland); they are required to allow citizens to form parties to further this aim; they are required to allow the issue to pass through all the phases of the standard British democratic process. If there is a constitutional procedure for the calling of referenda on important issues, then they are required to allow the pro-independence lobby to attempt to call out a referendum, and so on.

As I indicated earlier the mutual recognition of citizens is not merely a relationship between people within a given state, but is also a form of reciprocal recognition which citizens in one state give to the citizens of another. For me to enjoy the ethical standing due to a citizen, I need to have my citizenship rights recognized by my fellow South African citizens, but I also need citizens elsewhere in other democracies to recognize the independence of the democracy in which my citizenship is established. It is, for example, important that they recognize the democracy in which I am a citizen as a free state and not as a colony of some kind. The reciprocal recognition of citizenship across international boundaries once again places *procedural constraints* on how citizens might conduct politics with a view to rejigging the rules of association of our existing international order. The ethical constraints include the following:

- That the citizens in one democracy are not entitled to conquer, colonize, destroy, or in any other way damage the democratic polities which citizens elsewhere have established for themselves. This would be destructive of the ethical practice of democratic free states within which citizenship as a value is constituted.
- That where large-scale international constitutional change is contemplated (such as the formation of new confederations, federations, unions, international organizations, etc.), the political discussion of the contemplated changes and the political action which flows from the discussion must all be conducted in accordance with the democratic procedures established by citizens for themselves within their own democratic states. The discussion of the proposed new arrangements must be carried out by properly elected and accountable governments; they must be public; there must be adequate opportunity for the people affected by these decisions to make their opinions known through the normal democratic channels; and so on. Unilateral action by any party which does not show respect for the citizenship rights of any of the parties will not be considered legitimate within this international practice.

In summary, then, the existing form of the practice of democratic states is not sacrosanct. There is nothing, from an ethical point of view, which is intrinsically important about the fact that there are about two hundred states in existence at the moment. The existing boundaries are not ethically sacred and neither are the existing constitutional forms (union, federation, confederation or a consociation) of particular ethical significance. In the practice of democratic and democratizing free states, all these are possible subjects for political negotiation. From the ethical point of view, what matters is that the politics (discussion and action relating to possible changes in the basic rules of association) must be conducted subject to the constraints placed on civilians in civil society and the constraints placed on citizens in the society of democratic free states.

Realizing citizenship rights in democratizing states

In the preceding sections I have been discussing the relationships which hold between people who are participants, as the holders of citizenship rights, within the system of democratic states. I mentioned how such rights only make sense within the context of democratic states, which are complex legal systems. To be one who holds citizenship rights is to be one who is a primary constitutive component of a democratic state and is recognized as such, both within one's own democracy and by citizens within other democracies. We who recognize one another as citizens are people embedded in democratic states. For those of us who have the standing of citizens in democracies, this standing is of fundamental ethical importance to us. We would regard a return to the status of slave, subject or colon as an ethical reversal of major proportions. But what of people who are not yet holders of effective citizenship rights in functioning democratic states? What of those who live under non-democratic forms of government (authoritarian regimes, dictatorships, absolute monarchies, malfunctioning democracies, collapsed states and quasi states)? What conduct towards them would be ethical?

Let me start answering this question by making two preliminary points. First, let us recall that to be a citizen in a democracy is to achieve a high level of freedom. This freedom consists in being a member of a political entity within which the members have set the basic rules of association for themselves, in which the members continue to participate in a legislative process which makes laws to guide day to day conduct within the polity, and in which the members have available to them procedures for amending the basic framework of association. The democratic state in which this happens is itself recognized as free by other such democratic states. The relationship between citizens is diametrically opposed to that which holds in master–slave relationships. There are many permutations of master–slave relations which include feudal relations between lord and serf, some tribal relations between chiefs and tribesmen, many marriage relationships within which the husband is considered to hold property rights over his wife's person, offspring and material possessions, and many relationships between religious leaders and their followers which exhibit similar characteristics. But the master–slave relationship which is of most concern in this section is that which exists in states that are not yet fully democratic.

Second, in the contemporary world a vast number of people are participants in the practice of democratic and democratizing free states. Many live in states which may claim to be democratizing but which are, in fact, currently authoritarian states. Many people in such call for the abolition of this form of government and the introduction of fully fledged democracy. Well-known examples of this come from Sudanese people, Indonesians, South Koreans and North Koreans. Those who live in quasi states plagued with problems of corruption call for an end to corruption and the introduction of accountable government. Examples of this call emanate from Angola, the People's Republic of the Congo, Sierra Leone, and many others. Those who live under the yoke of dictatorial religious regimes look for liberation and the introduction of democratic practices. Such people are to be found in Iran, Iraq, Libya, Saudi Arabia and Afghanistan. Then there are, in many places, groups of people who claim that in the states within which they are presently located they find themselves to be the subject of ongoing discrimination and they accordingly seek to secede in order to establish a democratic order in which they will be free of this discrimination. Examples of states in which this is at present happening are Sri Lanka, Israel, Northern Ireland, Russia, Syria and Turkey.

In all these cases, my reference is to people who claim citizenship rights for themselves but who do not at present enjoy them in any real sense. These people (possibly a majority of humankind) are participants in the practice of democratic and democratizing free states. They demonstrate this in the language they use and the claims which they make for themselves, but for them, however, citizenship rights are not yet real, for they find themselves locked into non-democratic states of one kind or another or into democracies which are such in name only. Citizens in functioning democracies then need to understand that these people are not 'outsiders' in some sense hostile to the democratic practice, but are insiders attempting to make their rights claims real.

In the light of these comments, we can now return to consider how citizens in democracies ought to treat those who find themselves in polities within which master–slave relationships, such as those described above, hold. For citizens, what has to be avoided with regard to the people in such polities are relationships in which they find themselves in the role of master in a master–slave relationship. Thus, with regard to the states which are under autocratic, military or dictatorial rule, what citizens must avoid, amongst other things, are policies aimed at conquest and colonization; policies aimed at supporting the autocratic, military or dictatorial rulers; policies aimed at preventing the rise of democracy in those states; policies which seek to keep such states in permanent 'quasi-statehood' or which push them towards becoming weak states or collapsed states. All these are to be avoided because they make impossible the achievement of a *Sittlichkeit* within which the participants recognize one another as citizens in democracies.

In place of such policies, ethical conduct towards non-democracies must do whatever is feasible to foster democratic citizenship for the people in such states. *Only some very specific means are appropriate to the achievement of this end.*

Citizenship in a democratic state is something which, by its very nature, cannot be forced upon others, but has to be brought into being by a process of nurturing and education. It cannot be brought into existence through coercion. For, as was made clear above, citizenship in a democracy involves people recognizing one another as beings who together, as equals, are fit to stand for election to government office, are fit to participate in such elections and are fit to hold the elected government to account during its term of office. Citizens in democracies also regard one another as people worthy of equal concern and respect by fellow citizens and, a fortiori, by the elected government of the day. A practice of mutual respect of this kind cannot be brought into existence through the barrel of a gun. At best, what naked force may bring about is behaviour which pretends to be democratic.[24]

What citizens may do to foster democracy in places where it does not exist includes: not giving military and material assistance to those who actively hinder the rise of democracy (military rulers, juntas, etc.); denying legitimacy to such regimes; doing what is possible to legitimize the struggles of democratic movements against such regimes (provided, of course, that the methods such movements are using or proposing to use are not themselves such that they will hinder the rise of democracy); providing material support to them; playing an active role internationally to advance the cause of democracy in such states; supporting the civil society rights of all the people involved in the area; facilitating talks between the conflicting parties through first and second track diplomacy, and so on.

The direct use of force would only be permissible against aggression directed against the democratic practice – against, that is, behaviour bent on destroying the practice of democracy. But even in their conduct against such actors, citizens in the practice of democratic states are constrained by norms internal to their practice. For what citizens are seeking in the long run, even against those who are committing acts of aggression against the practice of democratic states, is to have the aggressor, him or herself, become a citizen who respects the rights of citizens in the global practice of democratic states in general. For this to come about, citizens must not act in any way which could be construed by the aggressor as an attempt to set up a master–slave relationship of any kind. Thus, citizens must seek to make it clear to the aggressor at every turn that any use of force would only be as a last resort, that citizens would prefer to use as the framework for politics, even with the aggressor, the framework of citizenship rights which citizens accord one another both within their democratic state and within the larger practice of democratic states.

In order to carry out the injunction of the practice of democratic states mentioned in the previous paragraph, citizens are obligated to treat opponents (those who do not yet claim citizenship rights for themselves) *as if* they were the bearers of citizenship rights.[25] What does doing this require?[26]

Citizens acting within the context of, and through, their respective democratic states would seek to:

- Make it clear at every point that their state respected all the rights respecting norms internal to the practice of civil society which is a precondition for the enjoyment of citizenship rights in the practice of democratic states. Doing this would involve them demonstrating respect for the normal set of first generation rights which civilians would take the aggressor to have.
- Treat the aggressors as people who could and ought to be self-governing in a democratic state. This involves not treating them as people to be made subjects, serfs or colons. This will involve using appropriate means – means which will not in any way suggest that what is being sought is a master–slave relationship of any kind.
- Create forums in which the aggressors could participate as autonomous self-governing-type actors. This would involve attempting to establish conferences, arrangements for mediation, consultative forums, and so on. It would also involve attempting to get the aggressors to participate in the forums established in the international organizations established within the practice of democratic states.
- Keep the political process as open as possible as is the requirement for politics among citizens within and between democracies. This would require of citizens that they take trouble to allow the aggressor to state his, her or their case as publicly as possible. Another aspect of this is that citizens would throughout any conflict encourage and facilitate the operation of a free press.

- Avoid at all costs portraying the aggressor as a generalized 'enemy' to be defeated at all costs. For what citizens wish for is not the defeat of some enemy, but the establishment of an ethical relationship with the people in question. This requires convincing he, she or them that they are not an enemy seen in some totalized way, but are rather a potential fellow citizen in the practice of democratic free states. Potential citizens are not to be treated as pariahs.

- Make it clear to the aggressors that what was sought was not victory, but mutual recognition.

- Make manifest that the shape of the arrangements in which citizenship would be enjoyed was not being prescribed, but would be the result of a political process. Thus, whether the people involved in the aggression would become citizens (in the global practice of democratic states) in one state or several, in a federal state or a unitary one, under a presidential system or a parliamentary one, all these things are to be determined in discussion with the other citizens involved in that area of the global practice.

A brief application of these insights to the Kosovo case

The ethical question which had to be answered in this case was, at its simplest: in the practice of democratic and democratizing free states how should citizens behave towards their fellow citizens in a member state in which the government of the day was behaving in a less than democratic way, in which a majority group in one of the provinces had started agitating for greater autonomy or secession, where the agitation had moved from mass non-violent action towards a more classic form of armed liberation struggle, and where, finally, the government had retaliated with 'counter-terrorist' methods which had all the hall marks of a policy of state terrorism, coupled with massive oppression?

Before answering, let me stress that this question was posed to all of us who are citizens participating in the practice for democratic and democratizing states.[27] It applies to citizens in states outside of Yugoslavia and it applies to citizens within that state too.

Applying the constraints mentioned above we get the following dos and don'ts for citizens wherever they are:

- Citizens should use the democratic process to support policies which overtly and articulately uphold the human rights norms of global civil society. This applies to citizens inside Yugoslavia and those in other states. This involves supporting the rights of civilians whether they be Serb, Albanian, or people from any other ethnic or religious group. Terrorist methods by the Albanian Liberation Front ought to be opposed, as well as the methods of state terrorism employed by the Yugoslav government. Citizens, understanding that a functioning civil society is a necessary condition for the establishment of citizenship rights, should support policies by their governments aimed at building the strength of civil society both in areas occupied mainly by Serbs and in areas occupied by Kosovar Albanians. Doing this would involve governments spending money building up private (as opposed to state) institutions such as schools, universities, organizations directed towards propagating human rights, providing legal aid to people being persecuted for political activity, and so on. This level of activity should not be directed at the formation of any particular form of governmental institution, but ought to be directed at the civil society itself, the society of individual rights holders.

- Citizens in Yugoslavia (from all its constituent parts), and citizens elsewhere, ought to support government policies which (both in their formulation and when put into practice) make it clear that they are directed not at conquering Serbs or at defeating Kosovar Albanians, but are aimed at finding an arrangement within which all the civilians involved can become citizens in functioning democratic states. The policies will have to be such that no party could interpret them as attempting to establish a master–servant relationship between one group and another. In particular, this would require citizens to have their governments avoid simply taking sides with Kosovars against Serbs, or vice versa. They would have to insist that their governments avoid language which extols one side to the dispute and vilifies the other. The policies should be aimed at preventing the abuse of civilian rights and at creating circumstances in which one or more democratic states could emerge.
- Citizens should be required to support efforts by their governments to set up forums within which the parties could negotiate *as if* they were already citizens of established states. Citizens should, for example, be supportive of the setting up of Ramboulliet type forums for negotiation, as well as attempts to use the forums available through the UN, the EU and NATO.
- Citizens ought to insist that their governments allow a maximum of political openness by insisting on freedom of speech, both within the disputed areas and within the practice of democratic states as a whole. Part of this requirement must be to insist on freedom of the press – demanding, for example, that reporters have open access to all the parties involved. Citizens ought to require their governments to object strongly to attempts to force people (on whatever side) to join political movements. 'Press gangs' should be opposed.
- Citizens should not tolerate attempts to portray one party to such disputes as 'the enemy' who is to be defeated at all costs. Thus, whilst a Slobodan Milosovic ought to be portrayed as a person who is guilty of a whole slew of human rights abuses, for all that, he was at the time still the elected leader of the government and a civilian with a full set of human rights himself. He was not simply an enemy to be destroyed, but someone who could in future become a citizen in good standing in the practice of democratic states. To have treated him simply as the enemy would have involved denying him ethical standing – treating him merely as an object to be destroyed.
- Citizens in their own conduct, and in what they demand of their governments, should make it clear that what is sought in such a dispute is not

victory for one side. The language of total war that was a component of a prior global practice is no longer applicable in the present practice. It is not victory that is sought, but a rejigging of the existing political arrangements which will allow everyone concerned to become a citizen in a free democratic state. What arrangements will achieve this have, of course, still to be negotiated.

• Citizens ought to make it clear to the civilians involved in the conflict area that no pre-packed set of ideas about the appropriate final political settlement is to be forced on them. It should be made clear that an appropriate outcome remains to be negotiated. It might consist of a single multi-ethnic Yugoslav state, or it might consist of a Yugoslav state divided along apartheid lines, or it might consist of a federation, confederation, or consociation. The possibilities are open. What are not negotiable though are: first, that the outcome must consist of a democratic state (or set of states) within which people constitute one another as equal citizens. Participants in the practice of democratic and democratizing free states will not accept as ethical an outcome in which an institutional structure is set up such that some master group (however defined, racially, ethnically, or in terms of religious affiliation) is set up to permanently rule over some slave group. The second non-negotiable position must be that the process of negotiation has to take place in a way which respects the civilian and citizenship rights of all the parties involved in such negotiations. The procedure has to be one which abides by the constraints of the existing practice. Thus, for example, the voices of the democratically elected governments in neighbouring states have to be taken into consideration and may not simply be ignored. No single imperial power is entitled to demand that its voice should triumph over the voices of citizens situated in other states.

Each reader must decide for him or herself whether in this case the conduct of citizens around the world and their governments lived up to what is required of them by the ethical model which I have put forward here. My view is that in large measure the conduct of all the parties involved in this 'war' were largely unethical.

Conclusion

In this chapter I outlined how our ethical standing as civilians is supplemented through our constitution as citizens. In it I sought to show how the standing we enjoy as holders of first generation rights in global civil society is improved upon through our being constituted as the holders of citizenship rights in the society of democratic and democratizing states. I concluded the chapter with a brief demonstration of the kind of guidance this constitutive theory might provide for those of us concerned with the question: What would it be ethical for us to do in conflict situations such as that which occurred recently in Kosovo?

7   Civilians and citizens

Compatible rights

This is a work of ethical theory in which I have examined the role of concepts of individual human rights in the practices of contemporary world politics. On the argument that I have presented, notions of individual human rights are not something marginal to the great events of world politics. It has been a central contention of this work that understanding many, if not most, actions in global politics in the contemporary world requires of us that we understand these acts to be situated in the two great practices of our time, civil society and the practice of democratic and democratizing states. I have argued that we only understand these practices once we have understood the rights claims we make within them and how these rights claims are internally related to the other major elements within these two practices.

I have argued that for those many millions of us who consider ourselves to be rights holders, these are the two global authoritative practices which are ethically foundational for us. Within them we constitute one another as rights holders and in doing so we establish ourselves as free people. In the first of the two, global civil society, we constitute one another as the holders of first generation rights, and in the second, the practice of democratic and democratizing free states, we constitute one another as holders of citizenship rights. These citizenship rights enable us to be self-governing in democratic free states in the wider practice of such states. It is as holders of citizenship rights that we can decide to grant to ourselves a further set of rights, the so-called positive rights (sometimes referred to as welfare rights), through the legal systems of our respective states. Here I have in mind rights such as the right to security services, welfare, health care, housing, pensions, and many other kinds of social services. It is only after we have constituted ourselves as citizens within the global practice of democratic and democratizing states that we may sensibly start talking of redistributive rights. It is only as citizens in such a co-operative practice of self-governing political communities that we can sensibly contemplate rights-based redistributions of our basic holdings.

At the outset I mentioned that a recurring ethical problem for me, and for others, is that, prima facie, there seemed to be a stark tension between recognizing all people everywhere as the holders of basic individual rights, on the one hand, and recognizing sovereign states within which people are constituted as the holders of citizenship rights, on the other. The tension arises because it would appear that states have a right to pursue their national interest in ways that often override the rights of individuals. This tension surfaces, for example, as soon as we ask ourselves what would count as ethical conduct towards asylum seekers, economic migrants, states which act autocratically towards minorities, states which abuse individual human rights within their territory, groups that wish to secede from one state to form a new one, groups which wish to carve out territory from one state to attach it to another, states which abuse the environment, states which harbour terrorists, states which fail to act rigorously towards international criminals, states which fail to uphold intellectual property rights of individuals, and so on. In each case we have to consider whether intervention by us as individuals in the name of upholding individual human rights is an ethical infringement of what appears to be a rival ethical principle which asserts that state autonomy is of fundamental value. In short, the problem is: how are we to think about the problem of individual rights versus states' rights? Alternatively put: how are we to think about the clash between our civilian rights and our citizenship rights? Is there a fundamental clash between these two norms? Or is there a theory which can show that both norms are part of a single coherent social practice or hierarchy of social practices?

The central thrust of what I have sought to establish in this work is that there need not be a sharp conflict between 'individual rights versus states' rights'. To put it another way, we do not have to make a fundamental choice between our rights as civilians and our rights as citizens. Instead, using constitutive theory, I have argued that we can best understand the rights claims we make by comprehending them as being embedded in two closely related authoritative practices, the second of which builds on the ethical statuses achieved in the first. In the first of these, global civil society, we constitute one another as *civilians*, the holders of first generation rights; in the second, the practice of democratic and democratizing free states, we constitute one another as *citizens*, the holders of equal sets of citizenship rights.

In the preceding chapters I have spelled out the major features of each global practice and elaborated on the relationships which hold between them. I argued that the ethical standing of rights holders, which we create among ourselves in civil society, while certainly of fundamental ethical value for us, is, nevertheless, when seen from a certain perspective, deficient in that the autonomy it realizes is still far from optimal. The very structure of civil society, while creating the status of civilian, which we value, also creates diverse forms of alienation – diverse forms of unfreedom between civilians. This deficiency has been remedied (or, in some cases, is in the process of being remedied) in that higher-order ethical institution which is the democratic state, which itself is recognized as autonomous by other such states in the community of states. Crucially, in this higher-order practice, civilians, without losing their civilian rights, are reconstituted as the holders of citizenship rights within democratic states in the system of democratic and democratizing states.

What emerged in the analysis is that in order to create a society of citizens in democratic states, the people involved must first be constituted as civilians in civil society. The enjoyment of the rights of citizen presupposes the enjoyment of the rights of civilian. To put the matter another way, the society of democratic states has to be built on the base of a civil society. *Thus it transpires that the rights of citizens which are enjoyed within democratic states are not in conflict with the rights of civilians, but are dependent on them.* Citizenship without civilianship is worthless.

What guidance does this analysis of the two great foundational practices give to rights holders as they encounter ethical problems in the international sphere? How does it help us get over the apparent tension which I have referred to so often in this monograph, the tension between individual rights and the rights of sovereign states? The analysis presented in this book suggests that whenever we encounter these ethical puzzles in the international realm there is a two-phase analytical process that has to be gone through.

First, as civilians (that is, wearing our caps as first generation rights holders in civil society), we must ask ourselves: 'What ought we to do under the circumstances to protect, promote and enhance basic first generation rights in global civil society? Second, in the light of the answer we have given to the first question, we must then ask ourselves, as citizens, as holders of citizenship rights in the practice of democratic and democratizing free states, 'What, as citizens, ought we to do about this matter, what constraints does our membership of this practice place on us?' Let us briefly consider how this two-phase procedure might work out in practice.

The civilian's answer

The general answer which a civilian must give to ethical puzzles as they present themselves is: 'I should act so as to respect, uphold and make real the rights of all participants in civil society. I should respect the claims of all those who claim first generation rights for themselves and respect them in others, and I should treat all other people *as if* they already claimed and respected these rights.' This answer means that, as a civilian, I should generally presume there exists a global civil society without any ethically relevant borders beyond the 'borders' which are constituted around individuals by the rights they hold. In civil society, people are free to use their rights to move about, to make contracts, to make friendships, to form associations for mutual advantage, to practice different religions, to speak freely, to study what they wish, and so on. They are entitled to do all these things subject only to the constraint that they recognize the same set of rights in others.

The 'only' in the previous sentence is somewhat misleading, for this latter constraint may prove to be very severe indeed. For any individual civilian will, of course, find themselves surrounded by other civilians and the congealed history of their reciprocal bonds created by the legitimate use to which they have put their rights. Thus, in seeking to exercise, for example, their right to freedom of movement they will find themselves confronted by, amongst other things, the property rights of others. Their right to move down a certain path might be blocked by another's right of ownership over that path. Their wish to exercise their right to buy an object might be thwarted by another's having bought it before them. Their right to enter into a contract of marriage may be thwarted when they find that the one they desire has exercised his or her own right to marry and has married another. In civil society all civilians are wedged into the vast and complex pattern of rights holdings set up by other civilians over time. Civilians always face the sedimented history made by others making use of their rights.

In the light of the above it may seem as if in civil society, with its tightly packed set of historical holdings, there is not much of a domain of free action for rights holders after all. To see it this way would be to miss the point. The overall ethical significance of civil society lies in the statuses which rights holders have to accord one another as they seek to make their way in the world. The key feature of civil society is that rights holders have to engage with other rights holders as people who have title to exercise vetoes in given domains as they see fit. To do this is to accord them a valued ethical standing.

What is particularly significant is what the constraints of civil society rule out. They rule out treating others as objects, who may, as it were, be ridden over roughshod. They rule out treating others as beings whose desires, wishes, and opinions may be discounted because they belong to a particular gender, non aristocratic stratum, ethnic group, national group, clan, or religious order, and so on. Most importantly, they rule out discounting a person's opinions and life plans simply on the grounds that the person in question is, or is not, a member of some or other political arrangement (a state, an empire, a kingdom, a *Volkstaat*, etc.). From the point of view of civilians, this kind of organizational affiliation is quite irrelevant to how a fellow civilian ought to be treated *qua* civilian. For civilians, these entities are of legitimate significance only if they themselves are the product of fellow civilians exercising their rights in accordance with the rules of civil society. Finally, they rule out using reference to the wishes of a majority as good reason to override the uses to which an individual has put his or her rights. Whatever my project in global civil society happens to be, the only ethical constraints on me are those presented to me by the rights of other individuals, and how they have used them, or not used them, as the case may be.

In order to illustrate this, consider, for example, the ethical problems which arise with regard to migrants, refugees and asylum seekers. From the point of view of civilians, there is no ethical distinction to be drawn between wanderers, tourists, migrants, economic migrants (whether they be work-seekers or travelling salespersons), refugees, religious pilgrims, students who journey in search of wisdom, and all other categories of people on the move. These are all individuals who have a basic right to freedom of movement. What distinguishes one from another is that they have different reasons for wanting to move from one place to another. The presumption must be that they are all free to move about the world as they see fit provided they have not (and are not) infringing anyone else's rights. *From the point of view of civilians, the general ethical judgement is that any civilian from over there (wherever that might be) is entitled to come to us here (wherever we are), to move about amongst us with a view to touring, learning, making friends, finding lovers, setting up commercial operations, praying with us, playing games, and so forth, provided only that they do not infringe our rights and the uses to which we have put them; provided, that is, that they do not seek to damage our rights of the person by murdering us, assaulting us, torturing us, preventing us exercising our rights to speak, to publish things, to pray to the God (or gods) we believe in, to steal our property, and so on.* In short, migrants ought to be treated first and foremost as civilians.

It follows from the above that in civil society, since it is a single society without borders, we civilians have to be concerned about the abuse of rights wherever they occur. There is nothing of specific ethical significance about those closest to us, which impels us to regard the defence of their civilian rights as paramount. There is, however, a practical constraint which is that we are often better placed to do something about rights abuses which take place close to us than we are to react to abuses far away. Civil society requires me to intervene where I can to prevent rights abuses. The possibilities in this regard are likely to be greater for me locally than they are in far-off places. In principle, though, the rights of all civilians, wherever they happen to be, are of equal worth. They ought to be respected and protected by civilians everywhere. In the modern world, with its plethora of technological innovations, taking on this task has become a lot more feasible than it was before.

The citizen's answer

For the holders of citizenship rights the general answer to the ethical question: 'What ought we as citizens to do under the circumstances?' is 'Act so as to nurture and advance the practice of democratic and democratizing free states within which citizenship, with its associated set of rights, is established as a valued form of ethical standing.' The meaning of this injunction needs to be spelled out.

First, when we are thinking of ethical problems from the point of view of a citizen, we are thinking about them from the point of view of one constituted as such within the context of one or another democratic (or democratizing) state. Thus, this question may be rephrased as 'As a citizen of democratic state X (for example, the USA), what should I do about Y (the treatment of refugees would be a good example here taken from the list of hard cases mentioned earlier)?' The question for her is about what it would be ethical for her as a citizen of the USA to do about the issue in question. She is thinking about it as a political actor constituted as such in this particular polity. This requires her to think of the problem taking into account her fellow US citizens, the government they have elected, and the policies that government has adopted.

Second, in terms of the analysis that I have given, we know that citizenship rights are only of value insofar as citizens are also concurrently *civilians* in the practice of civil society.[1] So, from an ethical point of view, citizens are required to respect and uphold the full set of rights which civilians enjoy. This means that as citizens we should respect the rights of civilians without regard to their place of origin. We should respect their right to be amongst us exercising their first generation rights as they wish, subject to the normal constraint that they respect the rights of others. What this means is that as *citizens* we should oppose policies by our governments which seek to deny to *civilians*, including ourselves in our capacity as civilians, basic civil society rights. This applies whether the civilians are Moroccans, Mexicans, Puerto Ricans, French, South Africans, or Brazilians. In terms of the analysis which I have offered, we should refrain from talking of refugees, economic migrants, asylum seekers, and so on, as if they were in some sense intruders without a warrant to move about amongst us in the domain within which we exercise our citizenship rights. The value of our citizenship depends on the prior existence of civil society, which transcends the boundaries of our particular sovereign democratic state. In civil society all civilians have a set of basic rights, including the right to free movement, which they are entitled to exercise as they see fit. The way in which we talk about our first generation rights and our citizenship rights can only be harmonized if we comprehend global civil society as the foundation on which the society of democratic states (within which we constitute one another as the holders of citizenship rights) is built.

Third, as citizens we are called upon to respect the rights of fellow *citizens* wherever they may be. In the practice of democratic and democratizing states our fellow citizens are not only those who are, with us, citizens in our own specific democratic state, but our fellow citizens are citizens everywhere, in whatever democratic or democratizing state they happen to be in the global practice of democratic and democratizing free states. *It is crucial to note that the value of citizenship does not only consist of the relationship of mutual recognition between citizens within a particular democratic state, but in the wider set of citizen-constituting relationships in the practice of democratic states as a whole. My citizenship is made valuable by being recognized not only by my fellow citizens in this state, but also through the recognition accorded it by other citizens elsewhere in other states.* Citizenship matters because, in recognizing others as our fellow citizens, we accord them that standing appropriate to people we take to be worthy of participating as equals in the self-government of the polity within which they find themselves. We take their democratic state to be of equal worth with other democratic states in the practice. As people accorded standing enough to be self-governing, they are not to be considered slaves, minions, serfs, children, primitive people (where 'primitive' is understood as 'not yet adult enough to be self-governing'), and so on, and their democratic polity is not be considered a subject territory, colony, dominion, etc.

Fourth, just as we need to give proper recognition to other citizens wherever they happen to be, so too do we need recognition from them. The superior ethical standing which we enjoy as citizens is only achieved when we are recognized as such by other *citizens*, either in our own democratic state or in some other democratic state in the practice of sovereign democratic states taken as a whole. From the point of view of constitutive theory, reciprocal recognition of our respective polities as *equal* is always at the heart of ethical relationships. What is to be avoided, what must be considered a major setback from an ethical point of view (from the point of view of this foundational authoritative practice), are other forms of recognition which fall short of this. The paradigm case of an unethical relationship relevant to this paragraph is that form of recognition which exists between an imperial power and a colony. This is a master–slave relationship which does not constitute the parties as autonomous. There are certain kinds of recognition which will not establish us as free. For example, it is ethically unsatisfactory from our point of view to be recognized by others as masters insofar as we are members of an imperial power, an ethnic group, nation or race, which group is taken to have a title to rule. To be seen in any of these ways by others is to be enmeshed in an unethical relationship with them. In short, we, as citizens, are called upon to actively pursue whatever lines of conduct are necessary to ensure that others do not see our state, in which we enjoy the rights of citizens, as the master state. In order to achieve this we have to ensure that the political arrangements established by our fellow citizens are such that in them our fellow citizens are constituted as autonomous. It follows, then, that where people in quasi states see the people of highly industrialized states as oppressors (according to some more or less sophisticated theory of neo-imperialism), this must be understood as an ethical setback for citizens in the industrialized democracies. For they are being categorized as 'masters' by people who, in some sense, understand themselves to be 'slaves' to an imperial power. Steps have to be taken to bring about whatever is necessary to nurture mature citizenship in the quasi states. For it is only after this has been done that citizen-to-citizen recognition of the required kind will come about. In some cases what needs to be done might turn out to be very radical indeed. I shall not go into the details of what dramatic changes might be called for, but the general thrust of the injunction which emanates from the practice of citizens is clear. The ethical standing we enjoy as rights holders in the society of democratic states depends on the other states in the society enjoying the kind of freedom which we value for ourselves in our own democratic states.

As just mentioned, the task for citizens when contemplating those in democratizing states where citizenship is less than fully realized is to foster fully fledged citizenship. This requires fostering a relationship with the people there in which they, as citizens in their states, recognize us as citizens in ours. Undertaking the task of building a constitutive relationship with others in which we constitute one another as holders of citizenship rights in our respective democratic states is likely to be very complicated indeed. This brings us to a fifth point which is that *only certain specified means will bring about this result.* Let us briefly explore this matter.

The use of force to bring about relationships of democratic citizenship is almost always ruled out. Threatening people with overwhelming force while commanding them to 'Recognize us as your fellow citizens or we shall got to war with you' will not bring the required form of recognition into being. It is hard to accept a state which has an army poised to attack as one which is seeking to establish a relationship of equality between its citizens and those in the target state. So, for example, the threat and/or use of force by one state against the citizens of a quasi state is hardly likely to engender in such people a sense that what is being sought is a relationship of mutual recognition between autonomous states. They are more likely to suspect an attempt at colonization. We as citizens, in discussing possible policies amongst ourselves, ought to be very suspicious of policy suggestions from our governments which involve the use of force to establish democracy in other states. For, in the normal course of events, to threaten force against people is not to accord to them the kind of recognition appropriate to those we hope to have as our future fellow citizens in a system of democratic states.[2]

Although the use of force is ruled out as an appropriate means to be used by citizens to establish relationships of citizenship with others who are potential citizens, it may very occasionally be the case, though, that those who have been denied citizenship by some, may have ethical reason to use force when seeking to reverse this denial. *If the excluded group have exhausted all the means available to them in pursuit of this end, and if it has no further options available to it to show that it is, indeed, in earnest about seeking citizenship, then the use of force may be justified.*[3] In practice, though, these circumstances will seldom arise – for it is seldom the case that a person or a group has no means other than force available to them to make the case for inclusion as citizens in a wider practice of democratic states. There are almost always alternative methods available which are to be preferred to force. There are normally other means available, the choice and use of which demonstrate a commitment to citizenship and democracy. Such methods include mass protests, stayaways, economic sanctions, strikes, passive resistance campaigns, and many different forms of civil disobedience. In deploying these means, those doing so can quite plausibly claim that the use of such methods demonstrates an ongoing respect for the targets of such campaigns – a respect which they hope will later translate into the mutual recognition which citizens in democracies accord to one another.

Sixth, in order to promote the practice in which individuals are constituted as the holders of citizenship rights within the practice of democratic and democratizing states, it is important to maintain an orderly system of internal border controls between the citizen-creating components of the whole. For, as I indicated in the previous chapter, part of the increased freedom which individuals enjoy as citizens is the freedom to be equal participants in the process of self-government within a constitutionally defined state or union of states – the EU is an example of this latter category. One of the benefits of self-government is that citizens can confer upon themselves sets of positive rights to services of one kind or another (education, welfare, health, etc). As I pointed out in the last chapter, a practical requirement for the provision of such positive rights is that the government of the day has accurate data and a measure of control as to who is in the state at any given moment. This administrative necessity, though, does not provide citizens in any particular state with authority to override the rights of civilians in global civil society. Citizens and their governments have no general ethical authority to exclude other people from the territory of their state. Quite the contrary, in terms of the analysis which I have presented, citizens are under a general requirement to allow civilians (from anywhere) to move about their territory at will in the exercise of their civilian rights. But border controls and other kinds of internal checks (such as the issuing of national insurance numbers) are required to ensure that the positive rights to the services that citizens have instituted through the democratic processes available in their states are enjoyed by the target groups specified.

Seventh, for citizens in the practice of democratic and democratizing states the highest ethical status is the 'citizen-to-citizen' form of recognition. The relationship is of value in that in it citizens recognize one another as beings worthy of, and beings who actually do, participate in self-government with their fellow citizens. It follows that if citizens from elsewhere, making use of their civilian rights to freedom of movement, come to live in our state and successfully form civil associations of many different kinds with citizens here without abusing anyone's rights, and without free-riding on the services which we citizens have provided for ourselves, then, if such citizens indicate a wish to transfer citizenship from their state of origin to our state, there seems little reason not to accommodate them. Should they prefer to go on living here while exercising citizenship rights elsewhere, that too is a choice they are entitled to make. But if such people wish to join our polity we should accommodate them. We should do this because we already recognize them as citizens in another state. In so doing we have already recognized them as persons whom we deem worthy of participating in a system of self-government with other citizens. If such persons are now living here with us and the government most pertinent to their day-to-day life is our government, then clearly we ought to allow a transfer of citizenship. By doing this we make their right to self-government real here where it most counts. If we were to deny such a transfer of citizenship in such a case we would effectively be restricting these people to the status of civilians in our state. We would in effect be entrenching a less than fully fledged ethical relationship between them and ourselves.

In this matter it is quite wrong to think that the question about whether to extend citizenship to citizens from elsewhere is akin to the question about whether to admit new members to an exclusive club. Allowing the transfer of citizenship in cases like this is not properly understood when it is seen as the granting of a favour or privilege to another. Denying it to another in cases where it should be granted (as in this example) is to restrict oneself to a relationship of unfreedom with the person in question. It is to restrict oneself vis-à-vis this person to a relationship which is in some measure a master–slave relationship. For, in the case I have sketched, we would be enjoying effective citizenship here where we live and they would only be enjoying the status of civilian here and the status of citizen in some more distant state away from where they conducts their daily life. As civilian they would not be able to constitute us as fully free. Only the recognition of a citizen enjoying real citizenship rights can do that. The recognition granted me by a civilian cannot constitute me as a citizen.[4] *Our own liberation depends on the establishment of effective citizenship for others.*

Concluding remarks

I have attempted to show that claims about human rights are central to *any* understanding of contemporary world politics. I was motivated to do this because, in general, human rights are accorded a marginal position within the discipline of International Relations and because even within that sub-field of IR, which is devoted to the study of human rights in world politics, a concern with human rights is not portrayed as central to the discipline in the way that, for example, states are.

Human rights claims are central for any understanding of our contemporary world because of the way in which concepts of individual human rights are embedded in the internal structure of the two major global practices of our age within which we are constituted as the actors we take ourselves to be. These two practices are global civil society and the society of democratic and democratizing states. No understanding of these, the two dominant practices of our time, is possible without some detailed knowledge of the role that concepts of human rights play in them.

This work has been an exercise is normative theory. 'Doing normative theory' is not an activity which is reserved for specialists, but is something we all engage with in some measure when we attempt to understand who we are and how we fit into the social arrangements within which we are constructed. We engage in normative theory when we seek to understand how we ourselves (and others) are constituted as the actors we understand ourselves to be within specified social practices. In particular, we are all normative theorists when we attempt to answer the question: 'What would it be ethically right for us to do in these circumstances?'

I built my argument from a starting point which takes seriously the claims of individual rights which I and many millions of others make for ourselves. We cannot make sense of the rights claims we make without situating them in the social practices which give them their meaning, just as acts such as 'scoring a goal', 'making a run', 'putting a king into check' cannot be understood apart from the games within which they are situated.

Starting, then, with the rights claims we make for ourselves, I outlined the contours of the practices within which these claims are located. I made the case that the first generation rights which we claim for ourselves are best understood in the context of a practice I have called global civil society. We, who claim rights for ourselves within the context of this society, I have referred to as 'civilians'. An important finding of this section of the inquiry was that we can spell out the major features of this practice in a way that makes no reference to the existence (or not) of sovereign states and without any reference to bounded territorial legal jurisdictions. Our first generation rights claims indicate the existence of a practice within which we make claims of right against one another which is global and borderless. Although states, with their associated legal systems and administrative machinery, might be instrumentally necessary to us to ensure the enforcement of our rights, we can understand such rights claims perfectly well without reference to such apparatuses. In Chapter 5 I discussed in some detail several of the rather extraordinary features of global civil society.

In what followed, I argued that our ethical standing as civilians, as holders of first generation rights, in global civil society is in many ways incomplete. It is incomplete in that in civil society we are in many ways alienated from one another. In the contemporary world, our remedy for its shortcomings has been to supplement our status as holders of first generation rights with another rights-based status – that of citizen. To be a citizen is to be the holder of a specified set of citizenship rights within the practice of democratic and democratizing states. In Chapter 6 I outlined the major features of this higher-order rights-based practice.

Next, I examined an apparent tension which often appears to hold between these two global practices. This is the apparent tension between the rights claims we make as civilians and those we make as citizens. This often manifests as a conflict between individual rights and states' rights. I then made use of constitutive theory to show how these two global rights-constituting practices could be shown to cohere. Civilian rights, I argued, are a requirement for the enjoyment of citizenship rights.

Finally, I briefly indicated how this understanding of these two rights-constituting practices may be used to guide us when we confront many of the ethical hard cases that are before us in today's world. Constitutive theory, as outlined, suggests to us that we need to confront such cases as both civilians and citizens simultaneously. We need to adopt policies that put into place the elaborate systems of mutual recognition that both require.

Notes

1 Introduction

1 An example here is provided by the hard-fought debates between Christian theologians for and against an understanding of Christianity known as 'liberation theology'.
2 Prominent modern examples of jurisprudents who have engaged in this kind of interpretive effort are Ronald Dworkin, Lon Fuller, John Finnis and Joseph Raz.
3 An example of the putting forward of rival understandings of this practice was provided in the debate in the USA about the place of the liberal canon in university life in general.
4 W. Dilthey, *Selected Writings*, trans. H.P. Rickman, Cambridge University Press: Cambridge, 1979; Ludwig Wittgenstein, *Philosophical Investigations*, trans. T.E.M. Anscombe, Blackwell: Oxford, 1963; P. Winch, *The Idea of a Social Science*, London: Routledge and Kegan Paul, 1958.
5 Timothy Dunne, 'The social construction of international society', *European Journal of International Relations*, vol. 1, no. 1 (September 1995), pp. 367–89. Martha Finnemore, 'Norms, culture and world politics: insights from sociology's institutionalism', *International Organization*, vol. 50, no. 2 (Spring 1996), pp. 325–47. Peter J. Katzenstein, *Cultural Norms and National Security: Police and Military in Postwar Japan*, Cornell University Press: Ithaca, 1996. Bruce Hall, 'Constructivism, sovereignty, and the methodology of hopeful non-determinism', paper presented at International Studies Association congress in Minneapolis, Providence, 1998. Christian Reus-Smit, 'The constitutional structure of international society and the nature of fundamental institutions', *International Organization*, vol. 51, 1997. Ammanuel Adler, 'Seizing the middle ground: constructivism in world politics', *European Journal of International Relations*, vol. 3, no. 3 (September 1997), pp. 319–64. Kathryn Sikkink, *Ideas and Institutions: Developmentalism in Brazil and Argentina*, Ithaca, NY: Cornell University Press, 1991. Jeffrey T. Checkel, *Ideas and International Political Change*, New Haven: Yale University Press, 1997. Alexander Wendt, 'Anarchy is what states make of it: the social construction of power politics', *International Organization*, vol. 46, no. 2 (Spring 1992). Cecelia Lynch, *Beyond Appeasement, Interpreting Interwar Peace Movements in World Politics*, Ithaca, NY: Cornell University Press, 1999. Audie Klotz and Cecelia Lynch 'Constructing Global Politics', unpublished manuscript, 1999.
6 For a discussion of the uneasy mix of positivist and hermeneutic aspirations in the constructivist literature, see Richard Shapcott, 'Solidarism and after: Global governance, international society and the normative "turn" in International Relations', *Pacifica Review* vol. 12, no. 2, June 2000, passim.
7 The circularity is illustrated in the following sequence of questions and answers: Question: 'What guides the behaviour of diplomats?' Answer: 'The rules of diplomacy'; Question: 'What are the rules of diplomacy?' Answer: 'The rules which are followed by diplomats'. When seeking to put forward an understanding of any practice

from an internal point of view this kind of circularity is unavoidable. In putting forward an understanding of a practice we can do no other than refer to elements of the practice that is supposedly being 'explained' by the understanding we are putting forward. What is taking place in such cases is not so much explanation as explication.

8 I can draw money from a bank, make a sale, write an essay, fix a lamp, run a committee meeting, make a promise, tell a lie, catch a bus, sing a song, etc. Each of these indicates my participation in a practice; indicates that when doing these my behaviour is subject to the evaluation of others in the practice; indicates that other participants in these practices are entitled to pass judgement on whether I have carried out these things properly or not.

9 By starting with an exploration of my self-understanding of myself as a rights holder, I hope to avoid any suggestion of my being an objective observer who in some way stands apart from the social phenomena being observed. I am speaking as a participant in a given set of practices and I am addressing myself to my co-participants.

10 This is a list of what have come to be known as negative liberties. They are also often referred to as first generation rights. It is not a complete list and I am not sure what would constitute a complete list. There is much room for argument here. We rights holders argue amongst ourselves about this. Many of us consider ourselves to have second and third generation rights as well as the rights listed. I shall not discuss these now, but for the moment I shall concentrate on first generation rights. I do this for these are the rights which can be conceived of as existing independently of any particular polity, state or system of states. In sharp contrast, second generation rights, the so-called 'welfare rights', such as the right to life, housing, healthcare, old age provision, education, and so on, all presuppose the existence of some or other public authority within an established polity against which such welfare rights can be claimed. This public authority need not be a state but could take any number of forms. In like fashion, claims of third generation rights are always claims made for the establishment of a sovereign state within which the nation can be self-determining, or for the granting of autonomy to the nation or ethnic unit within some existing state.

11 In what follows, I fully accept that 'identities are emergent and constructed (rather than fixed and natural), contested and polymorphic (rather than unitary and singular), and interactive and process-like (rather than static and essence-like)' (Yosef Lapid and Friedrich Kratochwil (eds) *The Return of Culture and Identity*, Boulder: Lynne Rienner, 1996, p.8).

12 Amartya Sen, 'Human rights and Asian values', edited by Joel Rosenthal in *Ethics and International Affairs*, Washington DC: Georgetown University Press, 1999, p. 189.

13 As is the case in Somalia at present.

14 Since the vast majority of states belong to the UN, this category includes the bulk of humankind.

15 It is important that I should not be misunderstood here. Although I know that a great number of people worldwide take themselves to have rights and/or act in ways that are congruent with such a belief, and, although I am confident that those who read this book are in all probability members of this group, I fully acknowledge that there may well be some who positively do not claim any basic individual rights for themselves. In this work I am not addressing myself to such people at all. I am not wanting to put the case that such people do, indeed, have basic rights but have simply failed to realize this. In like manner, in this work I am not attempting to convert to a rights-based philosophy of life those who believe themselves to be rightsless. But I would mention, in passing, that it is often the case that it is not those who are supposedly happy with their rightsless status who profess their contentment with this state of affairs. In many cases claims about the contentment of people regarded as rightsless people are made by others (patriarchs, tribal leaders, religious leaders, and the like) who claim to speak for those to whom rights are denied.

16 Indeed, it is difficult to imagine what a commitment to second generation rights would entail in the absence of a prior commitment to first generation rights. What would the value of a right to welfare be in the absence of the standard set of rights of the person such as those listed above? I cannot imagine setting store, for example, to a right to healthcare in the absence of the rights not to be killed, assaulted, tortured, and so on through the list adumbrated above. If the rights of the person are not secured, what point would there be in welfare provisions? Similar points could be made with regard to all the other welfare rights.

17 Simon Chesterman, 'Human rights as subjectivity: The age of rights and the politics of culture', *Millennium: Journal of International Studies* vol. 27, no. 1, 1998, pp. 97–118.

18 Michael Walzer (ed.), 'Introduction', in *Toward a Global Civil Society*, Oxford: Berghan Books, 1995.

19 Justin Rosenberg, *The Empire of Civil Society*, London: Verso, 1994.

20 Martin Shaw, 'Civil society and global politics', *Millennium: Journal of International Studies* vol. 23, no. 3 (Winter 1994), pp. 647–68. Jan Aart Scholte, 'Civil society and the International Monetary Fund', conference presentation, Netherlands, 1998. Michael Walzer, 'The idea of civil society', *Dissent*, Spring 1991. Alejandro Colás, 'The promises of international civil society', *Global Society* vol. 11, no. 3, pp. 261–78, September 1997. Ian Clark, *Globalization and Fragmentation: International Relations in the Twentieth Century*, Oxford: Oxford University Press, 1997.

21 There is a large literature which considers the merits of different forms of democratic arrangements. In it evaluative comparisons are drawn between representative democracies and participatory democracies, between republican forms of government and constitutional monarchies, between unitary arrangements and federal ones, and so on. I am not concerned with the merits of these, but merely to point out that all theories of democracy are built on the notion that a democracy consists of citizens who have certain democratic rights vis-à-vis each other and vis-à-vis the state in which they are citizens. These rights are ones which have to be understood as pertaining within some or other democratic polity, normally a state. For an overview of democratic theory, see J.R. Pennock, *Democratic Political Theory*, Princeton: Princeton University Press, 1979.

22 Of course, the scale and importance of our participation in world affairs varies from person to person. Nelson Mandela, as an elder statesman, does what he can to bring peace to the Southern African region. Key players in Norway attempt to broker peace in the Middle East through devices such as the 'Oslo Channel'. In the ongoing dispute in Palestine, the roles of Ariel Sharon and Yasar Arafat are more important than yours or mine. Yet the general point stands, that in the modern world almost everybody is a participant in some practices which are in some measure international.

23 Even were I not to do anything, what I think about these matters forms part of that hard to define, but very powerful, force known as 'public opinion' which often has a measurable effect on the behaviour of politicians.

24 As already indicated, I take the society of democratic and democratizing states to include almost all states. There are few states any longer which are publicly committed to feudal, absolutist, aristocratic, or authoritarian forms of government. Those few which are, such as the monarchy in Swaziland, have grafted on to the monarchical form of government strong democratic components. The public philosophy of the vast majority of states is democratic. Many of those states which are not yet practising democracies are committed to becoming so. It may well be the case that the governments of some states profess democratic commitments, but are hypocritical in doing so. But even the hypocritical usage of a justification depends on there being a widespread non-hypocritical usage of the justification in question. The existence of hypocrites is proof positive of a widely accepted standard of conduct.

25 See Mervyn Frost, *Ethics in International Relations: A Constitutive Theory*, Cambridge: Cambridge University Press, 1996.

26 The point which I make here is distinct from that made by Michael Cox in 'Social forces, states and world orders: beyond international relations theory', *Millennium: Journal of International Studies*, vol. 10, no. 2 (Summer 1981), pp. 126–155.

27 Note that a constitutive norm of the Klu Klux Klan is that members are required to hate (or a least act as if they hate) blacks. Thus unethical conduct within the context of this practice would be conduct which flouted this constitutive norm. On the view which I am putting forward, then, what is to count as ethical is determined by the constitutive norms internal to a given practice.

28 It is important to note that there is a very strong sense in which the constitutive norms of a given practice are *foundational* for that practice. One's standing as a participant within in a practice is founded on one's adherence to these foundational norms. However, the notion that the constitutive norms are foundational in no way indicates that they hold some kind of special metaphysical status as ultimately true, beyond doubt and valid for all time. It is self-evident that the constitutive norms of practices evolve and change. Invariably standards of ethical conduct within a given practice change with time.

29 It is important for my argument to note that pointing out instances of failure to adhere to the constitutive rules of a practice (thus opening the actors in question to ethical criticism) does not necessarily prove that the constitutive standard does not exist. Thus, for example, pointing out that some people in the practice of academic life knowingly propagate falsehoods does not prove that within this practice truth-telling is not a fundamental constitutive norm.

2 Individual rights in world politics: central not marginal

1 A. Buchanan, *Secession: The Morality of Political Divorce*, Boulder: Westview Press, 1991. Mervyn Frost, 'Migrants, civil society and sovereign states: Investigating an ethical hierarchy', *Political Studies* vol. 46, no. 5, December 1998, pp. 71–85.

2 On the clash between global solidarities and particularist loyalties, see C. Brown, 'International relations theory and the idea of world community', Ken Booth and Steven Smith (eds) *International Relations Theory Today*, Cambridge: Polity Press, 1995.

3 Richard Mansbach, *The Global Puzzle: Issues and Actors in World Politics*, 2nd edn, Boston: Houghton Mifflin, 1997.

4 Richard Little and M. Smith (eds) *Perspectives in World Politics*, 2nd edn, London: Routledge, 1991.

5 Paul R. Viotti and Mark V. Kauppi, *International Relations Theory: Realism, Pluralism and Globalism*, New York: Macmillan, 1993.

6 H. Bull, *The Anarchical Society*, London: Macmillan, 1977. Hans Morgenthau, *Politics Among Nations*, New York: Knopf, 1973.

7 H. Bull, 'Human rights and world politics', in R. Pettman (ed.) *Moral Claims in World Affairs*, London, Croom Helm, 1979.

8 Mervyn Frost, 'A turn not taken: Ethics in IR at the millennium', *Review of International Studies*, vol. 24, Special Issue on *The Eighty Years Crisis 1919–1999*, December 1998, pp. 119–32.

9 Justin Rosenberg, 'What's the matter with realism?', in *Review of International Studies* vol. 16, no. 4, October 1990, pp. 285–303.

10 Jack Donnelly, *Universal Human Rights in Theory and Practice*, Ithaca, NY: Cornell University Press, 1989. David P. Forsyth, *Human Rights and World Politics*, Lincoln/London: University of Nebraska Press, 1989. John Galtung, *Human Rights in Another Key*, Cambridge: Polity Press, 1994. Barbara Johnson (ed.), *Freedom and Interpretation: The Oxford Amnesty Lectures 1992*, New York: Basic Books, 1993. Henry Shue, *Basic Rights, Subsistence, Affluence and US Foreign Policy*, Princeton: Princeton University Press, 1980. L. Tagni, *The Struggle for Human Rights: An International Perspective*,

Kenwyn: Juta and Company, 1994. John Vincent, *Human Rights and International Relations*, Cambridge: Cambridge University Press, 1995.

11 What follows is a brief account of how I interpret what it is to have a right. For my purposes I do not need to enter into the hotly contested and ongoing debate about the precise nature of rights claims. For an overview of the debate, see David P. Forsythe, *Human Rights in International Relations*, Cambridge: Cambridge University Press, 2000, ch. 2.

12 Wesley N. Hohfeld, *Fundamental Legal Conceptions as Applied in Judicial Reasoning and Other Essays*, W.W. Cook (ed.) New Haven, Conn: Princeton University Press, 1919.

13 Hillel Steiner, *An Essay on Rights*, Blackwell: Oxford, 1994, pp. 54–108.

14 For a brief discussion of the history of human rights, see John Vincent, *Human Rights and International Relations*, Cambridge: Cambridge University Press, 1995, pp. 19–36.

15 Ronald Dworkin, 'Is there a right to pornography?', in *Oxford Journal of Legal Studies*, vol.,1, 1981, pp. 177–212.

16 For example, the populace might want to extradite you to some small island. The people cite as their reason for doing this that the common good will be served by your removal. Your removal will facilitate the sale of weapons to some state. Against this you claim a right to asylum. Here you bring out your right to trump the other reasons for action put forward in this case.

17 I have discussed most of these in some detail in Mervyn Frost, *Ethics in International Relations: A Constitutive Theory*, Cambridge: Cambridge University Press, 1996, Part 1. It is, though, important briefly to mention them here again.

18 This approach also exerts a strong influence on other ways of doing IR. These include the English School, Interdependence theory, Neo-Liberal Institutional theory and even Marxian structural approaches.

19 For a general outline of the tenets of realism, see Paul R.Viotti, and Mark V. Kauppi, *International Relations Theory: Realism, Pluralism and Globalism*, New York: Macmillan, 1993, ch. 2.

20 See Charles Taylor, 'Neutrality in political science', in *The Philosophy of Social Explanation*, A. Ryan (ed.) London: Oxford University Press, 1969.

21 As an example of such a state centric theorist, see, for example, H. Bull, *The Anarchical Society*, Macmillan: London, 1977.

22 The widely known definition of statehood fits neatly with the account of the state I have given here. This is the definition offered by Max Weber according to which the state is that organization which 'successfully claims the monopoly of the legitimate use of physical force'. Max Weber, *Essays in Sociology*, London: Kegan Paul, Trench, Trubner, 1946, p. 78.

23 Steven Lukes, *Power: A Radical View*, London: Macmillan, 1974.

24 Kenneth Waltz, *Theory of International Politics*, London: Addison-Wesley, 1979. V.I. Lenin, 'Imperialism the highest stage of capitalism', in *Selected Works of Lenin*, Moscow: Progress Publishers, 1977.

25 The dominance of this understanding of law is closely linked to the dominance of state-centric paradigms and the dominant understandings of power considered in the previous section.

26 A classic statement of legal positivism is to be found in John Austin, *The Province of Jurisprudence Determined*, London: Weidenfeld and Nicolson, London, 1954.

27 For a critical discussion of legal positivism, see H.L.A. Hart, *The Concept of Law*, Oxford: Oxford University Press, 1961.

28 For an expression of this point of view, see the excerpt by Jeremy Bentham in Jeremy Waldron (ed.) *Nonsense Upon Stilts: Bentham, Burke and Marx on the Rights of Man*, London: Methuen, 1987.

29 Thomas Hobbes, *Leviathan*, London: Dent, 1962, ch. 17.

30 See the discussion about the nature of international law in H.L.A. Hart, *op. cit.*, the final chapter.

31 I am not going to present the arguments which post-modern theorists have put forward for these positions. Their arguments are diverse and complicated. I simply wish to point to this as a position common to all post-modern theorists. For an overview, see P. Rosenau, 'Once again into the fray: International relations confronts the humanities', *Millennium: Journal of International Studies*, vol. 19, no. 1, Spring 1990, pp. 83–110.

32 Steven Smith, Ken Booth and Marysia Zalewski (eds), *International Theory: Positivism and Beyond*, Cambridge: Cambridge University Press, 1996.

33 On special obligations, see James Fishkin, 'Theories of justice in international relations: The limits of liberal theory', in *Ethics and International Affairs*, Anthony Ellis (ed.) Manchester: Manchester University Press, 1986.

34 For those not familiar with cricket or soccer, most other games will provide analogies which will do just as well, e.g. the relationship between moving a pawn in the game of chess to the other elements in that game, such as 'moving a king', 'moving into check' and 'checkmate', or the relationship between 'scoring a try' to the other core elements in the game of rugby, such as 'kicking for touch' or 'making a set scrum'. The central point is the obvious one that the item in question is an essential component of the *internal logic* of the game in question and that an understanding of this logic requires of us that we understand the rules governing the interrelationships between the core elements of the game in question.

35 For a discussion of the distinction between these two concepts, see Martin Hollis and Steve Smith, *Explaining and Understanding International Relations*, Oxford: Clarendon Press, 1990.

36 To ensure that I am not rigging the argument by carefully choosing appropriate examples, I invite you, the reader, to choose for yourself examples of important events in international relations which IR theorists ought to explain. Having done this, check for yourselves whether the arguments I make about the examples I have chosen apply to those you have picked.

37 I am aware that Kuwait was not a democracy at the time, but the allies understood themselves to be defending the rights of Kuwaiti people to establish self-rule for themselves, a right to reject conquest and to reject the tyrannical rule which would have followed such conquest. The international coalition against Iraq did not claim, for example, that what was being protected was the right of a king to rule his subjects, or a feudal lord to rule his vassals.

38 This understanding of what was taking place there has been challenged. It is often suggested that the account I have given is a mere rationalization, disguising the pursuit of naked self-interest by the USA and its allies (in this case, a real interest in the security of the oil supply from the region). But even this claim (that it, the rights-based account, is a mere rationalization) depends for its force on the presumption that the USA had a good understanding of the practice of rights and was thus able to use this understanding hypocritically. Hypocrisy always, as it were, rides on the back of a non-hypocritical practice. In short, nowadays the alternative 'realist' understanding is parasitic on a discourse about rights. Only those who understand the human rights-based view of the practice of states are able to engage in hypocritical action. The 'hypocritcal realist' account must finally be understood as endorsing the rights-based account which I am presenting here.

39 In other words, he understood the self-description of the act offered by the UN forces, but, having understood it, he did not accept it. He understood that this was how those who were attacking him thought. Against the interpretation of his attackers he presented an alternative account which stressed that the Iraqi people had a legitimate claim to the Kuwaiti territory. But this account, too, depends on notions about the rights of the Iraqi people.

40 Thomas Franck, 'The emerging right to democratic government', in *American Journal of International Law*, vol. 86, no. 1, January 1992.

41 Thomas M. Franck, *The Empowered Self: Law and Society in the Age of Individualism*, Oxford: Oxford University Press, 1999, pp. 53–5.

42 These rights are spelled out in the Geneva Conventions of 1949 which are, in turn, derived from the tradition of just war theory.

43 Michael Walzer, *Just and Unjust Wars: A Moral Argument with Historical Illustrations*, Harmondsworth: Penguin, 1980, passim. Richard Norman, *Ethics Killing and War*, Cambridge: Cambridge University Press, 1995.

44 Marxist forms of analysis – which allege that the free market system, and the justifications that its protagonists produce for it, hides an exploitative system – can only make such claims *after* they have understood how the free market itself works – that is, after they have understood the self-understandings of those who participate in it; only after they have understood the rules which constitute this practice. Before they can introduce arguments which profess to show that the participants are (mis)guided by ideology, they have to understand how the participants themselves understand what they are doing. To do this they need to understand the notions of private property, money, banking, profit, interest and contract, to mention but a few of the core elements in a free market practice. In sum, critique is always a second-order activity based on an understanding of a first-order practice.

45 David Campbell, 'MetaBosnia: Narratives of the Bosnian war', *Review of International Studies*, vol. 24, no. 2, April 1998, pp. 261–82.

46 For a particularly harrowing account of mass rape in the region, see Katharine McKinnon's chapter in Stephen Shute and Susan Hurley (eds) *On Human Rights*, New York: Basic Books, 1993.

47 It is not so much a linear argument as a set of arguments which thrust in the same direction.

48 The African National Congress in South Africa, for example, used a human rights approach to criticize the positive law established by the apartheid regime.

49 Jack Donnelly, 'Post-cold war reflections on the study of international human rights', in Joel Rosenthal (ed.) *Ethics and International Affairs: A Reader*, Washington DC: Georgetown University Press, 1999, pp. 242–70.

50 Frances Harbour, 'Basic moral values: A shared core', in Joel Rosenthal, *op cit.*, pp. 103–24.

51 John Finnis, *Natural Law and Natural Rights*, Oxford: Oxford University Press, 1980.

52 Michael Donelan, *Elements of International Political Theory*, Oxford: Oxford University Press, 1990.

53 This is illustrated in the following claim and counter-claim. The British Foreign Secretary claimed on 23 September 1997 that the sentence imposed by a Saudi court on an English nurse accused of murder (500 lashes and eight years in prison) was not acceptable in the modern world. ('Modern', I presume, is to be understood as 'enlightened' or 'reasonable' as opposed to 'primitive.') The Saudi Ambassador in London queried the assumption that British law and the British sense of what is just is better than the Saudi one. This was arrogant, he said (interview, BBC, Radio Four, *Today Programme* at about 7.45am, 23 September 1997).

54 For a set of articles sceptical about the possibility of reason leading us to a single correct view of human rights, see Stephen Shute and Susan Hurley, *On Human Rights*, Basic Books: New York, 1993.

55 Richard Rorty, 'Human rights, rationality and sentimentality', in Stephen Shute and Susan Hurley, *op. cit.*, pp. 112–34.

56 My argument does not call for an objective search for commonalities across diverse practices, but rather refers to the self-understandings which people from a range of different practices have about what pertains in an overarching practice within which they are all participating. A simple example of such a common practice is found in international soccer leagues where people from diverse political, religious and cultural

backgrounds participate together in the internationally understood practice of playing soccer.

57 A participant in these practices trying to disavow a concern with human rights would be akin to an avid chess player systematically flouting the rules of the game and thereby disqualifying herself from the practice of chess playing.

3   Foundational practices

1 Terry Nardin, *Law, Morality and Relations of States*, Princeton: Princeton University Press, 1983. Michael Oakeshott, *On Human Conduct*, Oxford: Clarendon Press, 1975, pp. 112–22.

2 An illustration of how different organizations may pursue the same purpose is provided by the many different organizations which have arisen with the aim of advancing the cause of human rights in world politics.

3 The UNHCR has been criticized precisely along these grounds for its handling of the refugee crisis in Zaire. See the report by Sam Kiley in *The Times*, Tuesday, 7 October 1997, p.12.

4 As I have already indicated, the way in which I develop this distinction is significantly different from the path taken by Oakeshott and then developed by Nardin. It would, no doubt, be an interesting and important exercise to detail and justify my account of such practices as compared to Oakeshott's and Nardin's view of them, but I shall defer that to another occasion. Here I simply state my preferred account as convincingly as I can.

5 It is helpful to consider the etymology of the word 'authoritative' here. It comes from the Latin *auctoritas* which itself derives from another Latin world *auctor* which means author or creator. These origins lead me to think it plausible to consider authoritative practices as practices which found or create categories of actors, set out specific roles for them, create sets of possibilities for developing those roles and put in place criteria for judging actors' performances of their prescribed roles within such practices. In short, authoritative practices create ways of life.

6 Many people allege that playing any game for the purpose of making money has the effect of undermining the character of the game.

7 The cricket association may be concerned to increase attendance at matches and by so doing to increase the takings at the gate, but, once again, this does not negate the cental point which is that they are guided by the character of the game – how might *cricket* be modified to make it more popular in order to bring in more revenue.

8 That a debate can be held about the merits (and demerits) of professionalizing a sport proves the point I am making. For what is at issue in such a debate is whether the pursuit of purposes external to the intrinsic value of the game sullies the latter, or not. The debate turns on the distinction between values internal to the practice and values external to it. A purposive association cannot be understood at all except with reference to the external purpose in question.

9 An example of this second kind of failure was provided by the fate of Hansie Cronje, the captain of South Africa's test cricket side, who was found guilty of 'match fixing' for money. He was subsequently expelled from the game. What he did was not cricket and he is no longer considered a cricketer.

4   Individual rights in conflict?: civilians versus citizens

1 The force of what I am getting at here can be illustrated by asking you, the reader, to consider the injury you would feel were you not recognized as having first generation rights, or were you denied citizenship in a democratic state merely because you were a woman, a man, a white person, a black person, a non-Christian, and so on.

Pointing to these foundational practices is not to deny the existence and importance of many other such practices. There may be many readers for whom the greatest injury would be, for instance, a denial of recognition as a Jew (a Buddhist, a Hindu, or as a member of some other religious group, and so on).

2 It is important to note that I am not asking how the foundational practices (within which I am constituted as the person I value myself to be) come into existence; I am not asking a question about the political history of these practices; I am not asking about the struggles which had to be endured en route to their establishment, or about the forms of power which had to be deployed in order to bring them into existence. In short, this is not an exercise in political sociology.

3 For example, if I happened to be a member of civil society and, at the same time, a participant in a purposive association, such as an association for the protection of wildlife that might call upon me to infringe people's individual rights in order to protect a certain species of wild life, then the rights-respecting requirement of the former foundational practice must override the dictates of the latter purposive association.

4 Here are further rather more fanciful hypothetical examples to demonstrate the point I am making. Suppose I claimed that my membership of the practice of bull fighting was foundational for me – that my participation in this practice was essential to my being the person I valued myself to be – and suppose further that, at the same time, I claimed my participation in an animal-loving religion (a section of Hinduism, for example) was also foundational for me, it is easy to see that the requirements of these foundational practices contradict one another. An objective observer would conclude that one of my claims must be hypocritical.

5 G.W.F. Hegel, *The Philosophy of Right*, T.M. Knox (trans.) Oxford: Oxford University Press, 1973. For an interpretation of Hegel along these lines, see C.D. O'Brien, *Hegel on Freedom and Reason*, Chicago: Chicago University Press, 1975.

6 What follows then is not a strict exegesis of Hegel's thought, but a rather loose and secular application of Hegel's approach.

7 In passing I might mention another practical association which is fundamental to our constitution as the people we value ourselves to be. This is the practice of friendship. Notice, first, that friendship can only be had within a practical association. It is not possible to create friendship through some purposive association with others. The values associated with friendship can only be had within the context of that practice which we call a friendship. Second, notice how friendship is fundamental to our standing as who we value ourselves to be. Consider someone who had never entered into a friendship – someone who simply did not know what is involved in being a friend to someone else. There would be a sense in which we would consider such a person less than a fully developed individual. Our sense of what it is to be a whole person includes the idea that such a person is one who is able to participate in friendships.

8 Robert Bruce Ware, *Hegel: The Logic of Self-Consciousness and the Legacy of Freedom*, Edinburgh: Edinburgh University Press, 1999, p. 176.

9 This list of first generation rights is not exhaustive. It is also highly contested, but this does not matter for my present purposes.

10 Robert Bruce Ware, *op. cit.*

11 Once again this sentence contains the circularity which is an identifying feature of all discourse about practical associations.

12 Note that as citizens our membership of this practical association (the community of states) is indirect in that we are, first, citizens of states which, in turn, are members of the wider practice, the community of states.

13 The point here is not that our involvement with these practices has to follow the sequence in which they were presented here, but that full standing as a free person requires simultaneous membership of all these foundational practices.

14 G.W.F. Hegel, *op. cit.*, para. 183.
15 G.W.F. Hegel, *op. cit.*, para. 199.
16 Convention on the Rights of the Child, United Nations General Assembly Resolution, 44/25, 20 November 1989.
17 These are not rights, properly so-called, for they may not be manipulated by the children as they see fit. We do not consider that children themselves may choose against claiming healthcare, education, welfare, and so on. Were these rights in the full sense of the term, they would indeed have such options. Rights, as I have defined them, have the character of trumps to be played at the discretion of the holder. Children do not possess rights, either negative or positive, in this sense.
18 John Locke, *The Second Treatise of Government*, Indianapolis: Bobbs-Merrill, 1952.
19 Joseph Raz gives an interpretation of a rights holding society as one within which diversity is valued for itself. See Joseph Raz, *The Morality of Freedom*, Oxford: Oxford University Press, 1986.
20 On the evolution of this sophisticated form of society, see Justin Rosenberg, *The Empire of Civil Society*, London: Verso, 1994.
21 Proselytizing religions such as the Christian religion are similar in this respect. They demand that all people be treated as potential members, irrespective of race, ethnic background, religious affiliation, gender, or class differences. This is the gist of the 'love thy neighbour' injunction.
22 This might be construed as an imperial imperative, but this is a misunderstanding insofar as civil society does not seek to subject 'outsiders' through conquest, but to attract them into becoming practising members by offering them direct experience of what being treated as a rights holder is like. Thus, for example, rights holders in contemporary South Africa, as members of civil society, are enjoined to treat women in traditional tribal systems as rights holders *even if such women do not conceive of themselves in these terms*. The rights holders are precluded from treating such women as the chattels of their husbands, as beings who do not have freedom of the person, freedom of speech, freedom of movement, freedom to own property, and so on. It is hard to conceive of this act of recognition by rights holders vis-à-vis traditional women as an act of imperialism. At the very least, an imperial act is one which forcefully imposes an unwanted order on the target of the imperial drive.
23 '*Baaskap*' refers to the status of 'Master'. In this case the 'Master' relationship was over 'Blacks' who were understood to be underlings.
24 Of course, many people who professed themselves to be respecters of human rights accepted the invitation and participated enthusiastically in the practices of *baaskap*, but by so doing they showed themselves to be but hypocritical members of civil society.
25 Critics may ask what the point is of distinguishing between the recognition we accord to fellow right holders within a practice from that we accord to those outside the practice who are to be treated *as if* they were rights holders. The answer is that making the distinction allows me to make it clear that talk of universal human rights is not talk which refers to some metaphysical feature (the possession of rights) which individuals are presumed to have independent of their participation in any social form. Instead it is much more prosaically understood as referring to a contingent social form which has arisen at a certain moment in history. The social form in question, civil society, has, as a component, an injunction about how to treat non-participants. They are to be treated as if they were already participants in the practice. No doubt this is done with a view to enticing such outsiders to become insiders in due course.
26 Were a number of us to find ourselves as castaways on an island, we could form a society in which we respected one another's rights without establishing a state, although reasons for the establishment of a state might well manifest themselves later. The way in which this might happen has been graphically described in Robert Nozick, *Anarchy, State and Utopia*, Oxford: Blackwell, 1974.

27 Robert Jackson, *Quasi-States: Sovereignty, International Relations and the Third World*, Cambridge: Cambridge University Press, 1990.

28 Two such enterprises are well known in Africa at present, Sandlines and Executive Outcomes.

29 This is precisely what dissidents in the USSR did for years, as did the opponents of separate development (apartheid) in South Africa.

30 Contrast the position I am defending here with that put forward by Thomas Paine who said that the state protects pre-existing rights and does not grant any new ones to its members. 'Man did not enter into society to become *worse* than he was before, not to have fewer rights than he had before', from Thomas Paine, *The Rights of Man*, London: Dent, 1930.

31 It should be noted that the precise form of government and electoral system varies from state to state.

32 The precise bundle of citizenship rights varies from democracy to democracy.

33 What is contentious about the goals of such movements is the way in which they seek to confine membership of such democracies to members of the nation or ethnic group in question. This is a problem for political ethics, but it does not detract from the general point being made here about the centrality of rights in contemporary notions of democratic statehood.

34 In this connection consider the almost unanimous criticism which has been directed at the regime in North Korea during the period that it has been an authoritarian state. The states of the present global practice have concentrated their efforts towards moving it in a democratic direction. Their efforts appear to have paid off.

5   Civil society: the space for global politics

1 The claim here is not that they are foundational in the sense that they rest on some indubitable and timeless ethical premises which are self-evident to all rational people. This is a practice with a history and our current theories about this practice are themselves part of the practice's history. 'Foundational' here refers to the role the practice plays for those of us who are participants in it. It is foundational in the sense that, in it, we participants come to have an ethical standing we could not conceive of having in any other way. It is also foundational in that membership of it is a necessary component of the hierarchy of practices through our participation in which we come to be the free individuals we take ourselves to be.

2 Justin Rosenberg, *The Empire of Civil Society*, London: Verso, 1994.

3 Michael Walzer (ed.), *Toward a Global Civil Society*, Oxford: Berghan Books, 1995.

4 Note that this category includes all of us, for in some measure we are all necessarily engaged in social explanation in that we all have some idea about what causes things to happen in the world.

5 Similarly, it would seem odd for the Pope to call in sociologists to deal with the ethical dilemmas faced by Catholic doctors charged with implementing birth control policies within democratic states. An explanation of the social, economic and cultural forces which produced Roman Catholicism will not determine what it is appropriate for a Catholic doctor to do in such circumstances. Likewise, an exploration of the discursive techniques used amongst Catholics to construct Catholic subjectivities would also not answer the normative questions posed to the doctors in such cases.

6 Mining exploration companies in Mali, for example, set up towns for their personnel which rely on the Mali state only for permission to conduct their explorations. For the rest, the companies provide all other services including protection, electricity, communication (via satellite), sporting facilities, hospitals, schools, clubs, libraries and housing. The rights of people in such enclaves are protected by the company, not by the state.

7 Put another way, one might say here, that this society is *open* to such a degree, that it extends the benefits of membership even to those who are not active members of the society. In other words, it does not discriminate in favour of practising members.

8 I do not think that there are many such people. I do not think there are many people who do not participate in civil society in any way whatsoever. But in spite of this, I think the argument about how rights holders ought to treat them is an important one.

9 As an example of such a relationship, consider that which held between the active members of global civil society confronting the ruling white elite in South Africa during the apartheid era. Here was a confrontation between active civilians, on the one hand, and a group of people who explicitly rejected social practices based on human rights, on the other. The rejection was based on religious grounds.

10 The international history of South Africa during the past forty years illustrates this nicely. Had the members of international civil society chosen to use force against those white Calvinists in South Africa who rejected human rights discourse, there is little doubt that a hostile polarization would have taken place which would probably have ended in open warfare. Instead, the international community treated this group *as if* they were rights holders throughout the anti-apartheid campaign. This modus operandi opened the way for this group to become active participants in civil society, and for these civilians subsequently to set up a democratic state which itself is committed to the protection of the rights of civilians.

11 This example is not really plausible because by definition civil society is not a territorially defined society. However, for the purposes of this limited section of the argument let us suppose that all participants in civil society are to be found within a specified geographical area and that all the non-participants are outside of it.

12 I must point out that the authors about to be considered did not specifically direct themselves to an analysis of civil society as I have presented it. Their concern was with the broad question: How ought we (who are constituted in one ethical practice) to treat outsiders? This may also be formulated as follows: What would count as ethical conduct towards 'the other' – towards those who do not hold our ethical beliefs – who are not socially constructed in the way that we are? A central aim for these authors is to question (to problematize) the way in which we standardly give ethical priority to the sovereign state.

13 Michael Ashley and R.B.J. Walker, 'Reading dissidence/writing the discipline: crisis and the question of sovereignty in international relations', *Alternatives*, Boulder, CO: Lynne Rienner Publishers, 1990. William Connolly, *Identity/Difference: Democratic Negotiations of Political Paradox*, Ithaca: Cornell University Press, 1991.

14 David Campbell, 'The deterritorialization of responsibility: Levinas, Derrida, and ethics after the end of philosophy', *Alternatives: Social Transformation and Humane Governance*, vol. 19, no. 4, 1994, p. 460.

15 Jürgen Habermas, *Moral Consciousness and Communicative Action*, trans. C. Lenhaardt and S.W. Nicholson, Cambridge: Polity Press, 1992. Mark Hoffman, 'Conversations on critical international relations theory', *Millennium: Journal of International Studies*, vol. 17, no. 1, Spring 1988, p. 91. R.W. Cox, 'Social forces, states, and world order: beyond international relations theory', *Neorealism and Its Critics*, New York: Columbia University Press, 1986.

16 Andrew Linklater, 'The achievements of critical theory', Steve Smith, Ken Booth and Marysia Zalewski (eds) in *International Theory: Positivism and Beyond*, Cambridge: Cambridge University Press, 1996, p. 212. Mark Hoffman, 'Critical theory and the inter-paradigm debate', *Millenium: Journal of International Studies*, vol. 16, no. 2, Summer 1987, p. 231.

17 Richard Shapcott, 'Conversation and coexistence: Gadamer and the interpretation of international society', *Millennium: Journal of International Studies*, vol. 23, no. 1, Spring 1994.

18 An example might be a nationalist involved in international negotiations who would not permit women from his nation to participate in such talks.

19 From the point of view of the actor, treating another as a rights holder and treating another 'as if' he/she were a rights holder are one and the same thing. The 'as if' merely signifies to the reader that the 'other' in question may be a person who does not normally conceive of him or herself as a rights holder and does not make the claims associated with this self-conception.

20 These rights lobbies have traditionally spelled out their role as being educative – as being directed to making people aware of the basic rights which they in some metaphysical sense 'already have'. This has often generated a hostile response because this formulation suggests that the target audience is backward in reason in having failed to recognize their 'natural' rights. Here I am portraying the activities of such groups in a different light. Treating non-participants *as if* they were participants is to invite participation. This is non-forceful recruitment.

21 Once someone starts producing arguments along such lines they are, in a sense, undermining their own case. The mere presentation of an argument would in a broad sense be an acknowledgment by the speaker that he or she has a right to freedom of speech.

22 Our ordinary language seems somewhat slippery here.

23 Note though that my argument in this book is that people who are completely outside of global civil society are likely to be few and far between. Although there are many people who belong to the kinds of practices which I have listed here, it is normally the case that they are also, at the same time, participants in some way in global civil society – most often through their participation in the global economic market, which is but one aspect of the society of rights holders.

24 Indeed, Carl Schmidt developed a whole social philosophy based on the bedrock distinction between friend and enemy. In my view, he failed to understand modern civil society which in many ways makes this distinction obsolete. See Carl Schmidt, *The Concept of the Political*, Chicago: University of Chicago Press, 1996.

25 This point is particularly pertinent to many people in Africa today.

26 Michael Oakeshott, 'The language of the modern European state', *Political Studies*, vol. 23, December 1975. B. Crick, *In Defence of Politics*, Harmondsworth: Penguin, 1964. Aristotle, *Politics*, London: Everyman's Library, 1973.

27 The same language is used in the 'stop/go' negotiations with regard to the future of Northern Ireland. Here we often talk of politics breaking down and the paramilitary organizations returning once again to the use of force. Finally, this use of the term 'politics' also fits the way in which we spoke of the breakdown of the political process with regard to the future of Kosovo before the bombing campaign started. The political process was one which involved discussion about the basic rules of association for the people of the region.

28 These are financial institutions which grant massive loans with which they seek to influence the direction in which the currencies of different countries move relative to one another. Their aim is to secure huge profits by influencing the direction in which the revaluations occur. 'Black Wednesday' in Britain is probably the best known example of what follows a successful hedge fund operation.

29 This is not to deny, in the least, that civil society itself is the outcome of a long history much of which was violent. How civil society came into being is a tale which includes references to key technological advances, to great political battles, to the decline of earlier forms of economic structure, to voyages of discovery and to historic revolutions. It is not my purpose to recount this saga here. For a detailed account, see Justin Rosenberg, *op. cit. passim.*

30 Attracta Ingram, *The Political Theory of Rights*, Oxford: Clarendon Press, 1994.

31 I must once again stress that we, who through the use of the language of first generation rights bring civil society into being, are often guilty of dramatic instances of

backsliding where we do not behave in accordance with what we profess to believe. We often fail to respect and protect the rights of others.

32 This might be a component of a much wider dispute in international relations about whether an international loan to a developing country ought to be made conditional on the adoption by that state of birth control programmes of one kind or another.

33 We shall have to await the flight of the owl of Minerva before we know what these movements of history produce.

34 Timothy Allen, 'Liberals, communitarians and political theory', *South African Journal of Philosophy*, vol. 11, no. 4, 1992, pp. 77–91. Molly Cochran, 'Cosmopolitanism and communitarianism in a post-cold war world' in *Boundaries in Question: New Directions in International Relations*, London: Pinter Press, 1995, pp. 40–53. Chris Brown, *International Relations Theory: New Normative Approaches*, New York: Columbia University Press, 1992.

35 For a detailed argument defending this position it is well worth reading Bruce Haddock and Caraiani Ovidiu 'Nationalism and civil society in Romania', *Political Studies*, vol. 47, no. 2, June 1999, pp. 258–274.

36 Robert Nozick, *Anarchy, State and Utopia*, Oxford: Blackwell, 1974.

37 John Rawls, *A Theory of Justice*, Oxford: Oxford University Press, 1972.

38 Robert Bruce Ware, *Hegel: The Logic of Self-Consciousness and the Legacy of Freedom*, Edinburgh: Edinburgh University Press, 1999.

6   Rights in the system of democratic and democratizing states

1 For a more comprehensive setting out of constitutive theory, see Mervyn Frost, *Ethics in International Relations: A Constitutive Theory*, Cambridge: Cambridge University Press, 1996.

2 A fine present-day example of this is to be found in South Africa where the citizens know themselves to have authorized the constitution in the founding election in 1994. The set of basic rules of association provided by the constitution is a set authorized by those subject to the constitution.

3 In seeking a solution to the problems associated with protecting and enforcing human rights, participants in civil society might get together to form protection associations with a view to pooling their resources to achieve this end. Initially such arrangements might be quite ad hoc, but with time the protection associations might become sophisticated with elaborate provisions for ensuring that the enforcement of the rights regime was fair. With this in mind the police function might be separated from the judicial function. All this might be placed within the context of an arrangement for changing the set of rules specially created to co-ordinate the myriad forms of associational life which rights holders might have created between themselves. In short, they might establish a legislature within a specific jurisdiction and in the long run end up with something like a democratic state. It would have been created as a purposive association.

4 Robert Nozick, *Anarchy, State and Utopia*, Oxford: Blackwell, 1974.

5 Andrew Linklater, *The Transformation of Political Community*, Cambridge: Polity Press, 1998, pp. 184–9.

6 I include here those states which we would recognize as established democracies and those which profess themselves to be en route to democracy. These two categories encompass the vast bulk of states in the world today. In this book I am not engaged in a survey to establish the precise extent to which democratic ideals have been realized in each state. My focus is on the ideas which underpin civil society and the ideas which underpin the society of democratic states and those states committed to democratization.

7 Thus the right to stand for election to the legislature is a right which a citizen may or may not decide to exercise, the right to vote may be used or not, the set of rights

designed to allow citizens to hold their governments to account may or may not be used by a particular citizen, and so on.

8   Thomas M. Franck, 'The emerging right to democratic governance', *American Journal of International Law*, vol. 86, no. 1, 1992, p. 46.

9   Legally defined states with these features have not always existed. As is well known they are a comparatively modern phenomenon. The history of this form of statehood is not my concern here. For an account of the rise of the modern state, see G. Poggi, *The Development of the Modern State*, London: Hutchinson, 1978.

10 I do not in any way intend this list of citizenship rights to be exhaustive. Precisely what rights citizens have will vary from democracy to democracy. There may be considerable disputes within democratic states about what rights citizens should be accorded. For example, a dispute might arise about whether citizens in a democracy ought to have a right to bear arms. In this work my concern is not with the details of the rights citizens have been granted in specific democracies. I am describing citizenship rights in general using a broad brush approach. A detailed study of citizenship rights in different democracies is a task for scholars in comparative law.

11 For a discussion of this issue, see L. Brilmayer, *Justifying International Acts*, New York: Cornell University Press, 1989.

12 H.L.A. Hart, *The Concept of Law*, Oxford: Oxford University Press, 1961.

13 I am well aware that with regard to specific competences the law of democratic states itself is taken to be subservient to yet higher levels of law. For example, the states of the European Union have conceded sovereignty to the EU on certain issues, as have the member states of the UN. This, though, does not detract from my present point which is that the citizenship rights which we currently enjoy are embedded in the legal systems of democratic states. I am presently engaged in exploring what this citizenship adds to what we would enjoy were we constituted as rights holders in civil society only. In the next chapter I shall consider possible ethical problems which arise with regard to democratic citizenship located in discrete states in this fashion.

14 Recent books dealing with this topic include David Held, *Democracy and the Global Order: From the Modern State to Cosmopolitan Governance*, Cambridge: Polity Press, 1995; Andrew Linklater, *The Transformation of Political Community*, Cambridge: Polity Press, 1998.

15 Whether our fellow citizens live up to this responsibility is altogether another matter. All that I am concerned to establish here is that, as citizens of a democracy, we consider ourselves entitled to call upon our fellow citizens in ways not covered within civil society.

16 All this is in sharp contrast to the circumstances which apply in civil society within which a fellow rights holder can approach me for aid, but I have no particular duty to provide it, nor do I have an obligation to provide reasons for my refusal. Charity may be requested, but we have no duty to respond to the request.

17 The sovereignty of the government in the modern world is not absolute, for it is itself subject to an increasing number of international laws and to the regulations of certain international (worldwide or regional) organizations.

18 Until recently this aspect of citizenship came to the fore most dramatically in circumstances where male citizens were called upon to risk their lives in war in order to protect their country. Women citizens have traditionally been called upon to make a different kind of sacrifice. On these traditions see Jean Bethke Elshtain, *Women and War*, Brighton: Harvester Press, 1987, and her 'Women and War: Ten Years On', *Review of International Studies*, vol. 24, no. 4, October 1998, pp. 447–60.

19 The point being made here might seem to be in accordance with the standard liberal interpretation of the state according to which the state is a device to protect pre-existing rights. It must be remembered, though, that constitutive theory moves beyond liberalism insofar as it claims that the democratic state is not merely a device for protecting rights, it is not merely a mechanism, but that it has a non-derived

ethical standing in its own right. The state has value as that practice within which the value of citizenship is created. It is that authoritative practice within which citizens are constituted.

20 Hillel Steiner, *An Essay on Rights*, Oxford: Blackwell, 1994.

21 Michael Walzer, *Thick and Thin: Moral Argument at Home and Abroad*, Chicago: University of Notre Dame Press, 1994.

22 What happens when we come to recognize one another as citizens within democratic states is that we accord to one another the status of actors of a certain kind within the context of a broad social institution. An analogy from sport is appropriate here: When we recognize one another as players of some sport, such as, for example, baseball, we recognize one another as players within that broad practice within which teams are the competing units. The status we accord one another does not depend on our being members of the same team. It also does not matter if the teams we belong to are in competition with one another. Indeed, in recognizing one another as baseball players we understand that it is an essential feature of the game that baseball teams compete with one another.

23 The public media (newspapers, radio, TV and online news) keep watch over just this kind of thing. We are regularly given reports about states which attempt to suppress opposition parties, muzzle the press, put off elections, rig elections, show themselves guilty of corruption, and so on. In doing all this the media shows itself to be a participant in the global practice of democratic states.

24 Conduct this thought experiment. At the point of a gun you are ordered to become a convert to Islam. The forms of behaviour required are explained to you. You obey. Are you now a follower of Islam? Of course not, for followers of Islam are people who freely follow the Sharia and who are recognized as doing so by their fellow believers. In like manner democrats are not people who are coerced into going through the motions of citizenship.

25 This parallels the requirement on civilians in civil society which we discussed earlier according to which civilians are to treat those not yet participant in the practice of civil society *as if* they were already participant rights holders.

26 It is important to remember at this point that the opponents of democracy being discussed here are likely to be few and far between. Most politics in present-day international relations is conducted in the language of democracy by people seeking self-determination in sovereign democratic states. Most people aspire to be citizens in functioning democratic states.

27 It will be posed again and again as this kind of crisis repeats itself in different places around the world.

7 Civilians and citizens: compatible rights

1 One can hardly make any sense of the notion of citizenship without presupposing that citizens have and enjoy the full set of civilian rights such as the rights of the person, right to free speech, freedom of the press, freedom of assembly, freedom of conscience, freedom to own property, and so on.

2 Once again, an analogy with the religious realm seems appropriate here. 'Become Christian or we shoot' is neither likely to produce Christians nor does it display a Christian attitude to the person or group thus threatened. The same point can be made with regard to other religious orders.

3 This produces the strange sounding maxim that only the very weak are ever ethically justified in resorting to force! For, by definition, those who are not very weak have alternative sources of power which may be deployed in such cases.

4 The example of South Africa under apartheid is pertinent here once again. The 'citizenship' enjoyed by white South Africans during the period of minority rule was ethically flawed. One of the reasons for this was that whatever recognition white 'citi-

zens' received from the disenfranchised black South Africans could not establish the former as citizens in the full sense of the word. The status of citizen (one worthy to be self-governing) is only valid insofar as it flows from the recognition of equals – from citizens like oneself. In South Africa, at that time, blacks knew themselves to be a subject people. At best, the recognition they conferred on whites was that of a subject towards a master. This form of recognition could not establish whites as free in the way that fully fledged citizenship now does.

Index